S0-BRO-054

GOD'S CO-OPERATIVE SOCIETY

SUGGESTIONS ON THE STRATEGY OF THE CHURCH

BY

CHARLES L. MARSON

PERPETUAL CURATE OF HAMBRIDGE, TAUNTON

Συνεργοῦντες.—2 *Cor.* vi. 1

LONGMANS, GREEN AND CO.
39 PATERNOSTER ROW, LONDON
NEW YORK, BOMBAY, AND CALCUTTA
1914

All rights reserved

GEN. THEO. SEMINARY
LIBRARY
NEW YORK

250.3R
M 3594

63262

GEN THEO. SEMINARY
LIBRARY
NEW YORK

GOD'S CO-OPERATIVE SOCIETY

Messrs. Longmans & Co.'s New List

THE BAMPTON LECTURES FOR 1913.

THE CHURCH IN ROME IN THE FIRST CENTURY. By the Rev. GEORGE EDMUNDSON, M.A., formerly Fellow of Brasenose College, Oxford. 8vo, 7s. 6d. net.

CHURCHES IN THE MODERN STATE. By the Rev. JOHN NEVILLE FIGGIS, D.D., Litt.D., Priest of the Community of the Resurrection. Crown 8vo, 4s. 6d. net.

EIGHTH AND CHEAPER IMPRESSION. IN ONE VOLUME.

LIFE AND LETTERS OF MANDELL CREIGHTON, D.D. Oxon. and Camb., sometime Bishop of London. By his WIFE. With Portrait. 8vo, 6s. net.

CHEAP EDITION, WITH NEW PREFATORY MATTER.

THE LIFE OF JOHN HENRY CARDINAL NEWMAN. By WILFRID WARD. With 2 Portraits, 2 vols. 8vo, 12s. 6d. net.

THE DEVELOPMENT OF ENGLISH THEOLOGY IN THE NINETEENTH CENTURY (1800–1860). By the Rev. VERNON F. STORR, M.A., Canon of Winchester, formerly Fellow of University College, Oxford. 8vo, 12s. 6d. net.

NON-COMMUNICATING ATTENDANCE. By the Rev. W. J. SPARROW SIMPSON, D.D., Editor of the *English Church Review*. Crown 8vo, 5s. net.

THE RELIGIOUS INSTINCT. By the Rev. THOMAS J. HARDY, M.A., Author of *The Gospel of Pain*. Crown 8vo, 5s. net.

CONTENTS: The Cry of the Hour—The Religious Instinct—The Interpretation of Instinct—Response—Personality and Miracle—Estrangement—Reconciliation—The Paradox of Christian History—Institutional Religion—Wanted, a Venture of Faith—Appendix.

VIA VERITATIS: Notes for Daily Bible Reading. Edited by the Rev. W. B. TREVELYAN, M.A., Warden of Liddon House, and the Rev. J. E. DAWSON, M.A., Rector of Chislehurst. With a Preface on the Devotional use of the Bible by the Right Rev. CHARLES GORE, D.D., Bishop of Oxford. Crown 8vo, 6s. 6d. net.

THE WORLD'S REDEMPTION. By the Rev. C. E. ROLT, M.A., Vicar of Newbold-Pacey, Warwick. 8vo, 7s. 6d. net.

This may be described as a serious attempt to set forth some of the fundamental articles of the Christian Creed in relation to modern scientific thought, the main idea being the inadequacy of the current conceptions of omnipotence and omniscience and the complete sufficiency of the belief that God is love.

A POINT OF VIEW: Addresses delivered in London and Manchester. By the Rev. A. C. BOUQUET, M.A., formerly Scholar of Trinity College, and Lady Kay Scholar of Jesus College, Cambridge. Crown 8vo, 3s. 6d. net.

JEWISH HISTORY AND LITERATURE UNDER THE MACCABEES AND HEROD. By the Rev. B. H. ALFORD, M.A., late Vicar of St. Luke's, Nutford Place, London. Crown 8vo, 2s. 6d. net.

LONGMANS, GREEN AND CO.

LONDON, NEW YORK, BOMBAY, AND CALCUTTA.

Messrs. Longmans & Co.'s New List

GOD OR MAMMON: A Counsel of Perfection addressed to the Clergy and Laity of the Church of England. By the Venerable JAMES H. F. PEILE, M.A., Archdeacon of Warwick. Crown 8vo, paper covers, 1s. net.

SCHEMES OF RELIGIOUS INSTRUCTION FOR INFANT DAY-SCHOOLS. Edited by Rev. R. W. BALLEINE, M.A., Diocesan Inspector for the Archdeaconry of Manchester. With a Foreword by the Right Rev. the LORD BISHOP OF MANCHESTER. 8vo, 1s. 6d. net.

SOME LOOSE STONES, being a Consideration of certain Tendencies in Modern Theology, illustrated by References to the book called *Foundations*. By the Rev. R. A. KNOX, Fellow and Chaplain of Trinity College, Oxford. Crown 8vo, 4s. 6d. net.

PRAYING FOR THE DEAD. By the Rev. R. J. EDMUND BOGGIS, B.D., Vicar of St. Mary Magdalene's, Barnstaple, North Devon; formerly Sub-Warden of St. Augustine's Missionary College, Canterbury. Crown 8vo, 3s. 6d. net.

CHRISTIAN PROGRESS, WITH OTHER PAPERS AND ADDRESSES. By the Rev. GEORGE CONGREVE, of the Society of St. John Evangelist, Cowley, Oxford. POPULAR EDITION. Crown 8vo, paper covers, 6d. net.

THE HOLY COMMUNION: A Manual Historical, Doctrinal, and Devotional. By the Right Rev. J. DENTON THOMPSON, D.D., Bishop of Sodor and Man. Fcap. 8vo, 1s. 6d. net.

GRADED SUNDAY SCHOOL LESSON BOOKS.

LONDON DIOCESAN SUNDAY SCHOOL MANUALS.

Issued with the authority of the BISHOP OF LONDON.

Editor—Rev. S. KIRSHBAUM, B.D., Hon. Secretary, Bishop of London's Sunday School Council.

FOUR NEW VOLUMES. Crown 8vo, **1s. 6d.** net each.

SIMPLE LESSONS ON THE LIFE OF OUR LORD. By the Rev. H. A. LESTER, M.A., Director of Sunday School Work in the Diocese of London, and Miss EVELINE B. JENNINGS. [*For Scholars* 8–10.

THE OLD TESTAMENT SUNDAY LESSONS. By the Rev. A. B. BATER, M.A., Principal of the Training College, Derby. [*For Scholars* 10–12.

THE BEGINNING OF THE CHRISTIAN CHURCH. By the Rev. Canon WESLEY DENNIS, M.A., Principal of the Training College, Battersea, and the Rev. G. H. DIX, M.A., Lecturer at St. John's College, Battersea. [*For Scholars of* 13.

THE PRAYER-BOOK IN THE CHURCH. By the Rev. W. HUME CAMPBELL, M.A., Principal of St. Christopher's College, Blackheath. [*For Scholars over* 13.

** *Prospectus of the Series sent on Application.*

LONGMANS, GREEN AND CO.
LONDON, NEW YORK, BOMBAY, AND CALCUTTA.

TO

THE BRAVEST OF CAPTAINS, AND MOST SKILFUL OF THE
SWORDSMEN OF THE HOLY GHOST

STEWART DUCKWORTH HEADLAM

THESE ESSAYS ARE DEDICATED

WITH THE AFFECTION OF AN OLD FRIEND AND COMRADE

PREFACE

ONE of the privileges of an English Churchman is that he is allowed to speak his mind with freedom, being well assured that, if he is listened to at all, he will hear in reply things equally outspoken, perhaps things even more tartly corrective and salutary. The author has risked some displeasure from his readers, if such there be, by a frankness, which to certain critics appears almost brutal. If the thoughts themselves are just, if they are so delivered as to reach the reader in the sense in which they leave the writer, they must be the apology. They will suffice. But a man who does not conceal his regret at much that he sees in the Church, nor shrinks from mentioning her diseases, nor dissimulates his terror at some palsies which threaten her, may perhaps ask for a patient hearing because he has not despaired of the republic. On the contrary, he has found his position, as one of the obscurer servants of the Catholic Church in England, to be satisfactory and joyful, even to the edge of triumph.

HAMBRIDGE, TAUNTON.
ST. LUKE, 1913.

CONTENTS

GOD'S CO-OPERATIVE SOCIETY

CHAPTER I

THE CHURCH OF ENGLAND : THE REFORMATION

IT is almost an ungracious task to attempt anything like Church defence, for the true and only safe Church defence is Church attack. The Christian Society, like the regiment in " The drums of the fore and aft," has not yet awakened to the salutary truth that " a Ghazi attacked is very different from a Ghazi attacking." The wild hordes are ceaselessly assaulting the Church, which Christ died to found, rose to enliven, and ascended to endow. They are formidable enough, but far less formidable if they are dealt with by assault, than if they are allowed the attack. The Church policy of the future should be such that we should hear much of the defence of atheism, the defence of Congregationalism, of Methodism, and of all other forms of individualism in religion, but little or nothing about Church defence. Such a policy, however, requires a different executive and a different strategic basis from those we now possess and are accustomed to.

The executive is mainly concerned with persons, and those persons are again chiefly the bishops. As long as our bishops are appointed by prime ministers of any belief or none, and are appointed with the first consideration

A

40

that their policy should be pacific, their warfare accomplished in their curateage, so long the Church militant will hold forts and man walls, but will remain ineffective in the conquest of the world ; and will moreover suffer the inconvenience of being a prey to any marksman who chooses to snipe at her sentinels. It is a curious evidence of how the world fears the Church to observe that, from the days of Wolsey to the present, the leaders of the State, and alas ! of the Church also, at their instigation, have resisted the need of extending the episcopate and multiplying dioceses. It is so easy, when bishops are so few, to select men who can be trusted to keep up a purely defensive line of action or inaction. The policy of Henry VIII is still the civil policy. That shrewd monarch would have none of Wolsey's enlarged episcopate, and the consequence is that most of our parishes are unvisited in a decade, many of them unvisited at all, and none of them are inspired and coordinated in a co-operative and pugnacious policy. The remedies for this deplorable state of things are obvious. The Establishment, an absurdity in a non-Christian polity and a disaster when controlled by mere statesmen, must be snapped from the limbs of the Church. The dioceses must be divided and subdivided. The bishops must be elected, as most of the bishop-saints in the calendar were elected, by the whole body of the baptized. The Christian battle must be re-ordered, with captains who are not merely gentlemen of personal probity but trained and scientific soldiers, who can plan wisely as well as fight manfully. These things perhaps belong rather to our children to accomplish than to ourselves.

In the meantime the strategic basis may be outlined and agreed upon by the communal sense of the Church.

The Church of England

It is not only likely, but in accordance with the history of Christ's Body, that the lines of action should be agreed upon by the informed whole before the execution of that action should be entrusted to the proper members. It is not to individuals that the promises of permanence and prevalence have been given. The rulers of the Church are rightly regarded as her servants, not as her masters. The democratic attempts to remodel the State are but hazy and often feeble attempts to carry out in civil life the doctrines taught by the Faith, and the grander Humanism of the Incarnation. We must not wait for the bishops of the future to choose our strategy, but only to mature and to order it and make it effective. Neither an autocracy nor an oligarchy will suffice. God's common people are the ultimate court of appeal, not some, not even one whole nation or one whole generation. The whole body of the Church is governed and sanctified by the Holy Ghost, and the rulers are delegates of that body, of all the nations and of all the centuries. Consequently our desires, the plans of campaign, and the strategy we approve, are limited by the demands of foreign Christians and past ages, for our bishops are not only our delegates but the delegates of the baptized through the earth and of the dead in Christ through the centuries. This means that our demands must be Catholic and they must be historic: or our delegates would be able to tell us that they are not the delegates of our whims, but of our Faith. Indeed it is just here that civic democracy is so weak and foolish. It has no continuity. It has no foreign policy. It has no Revelation to act like a centre of gravity, to keep it from the schisms of the centrifugal forces. Hence it usually passes into a despotism, as did revolutionary France, or into an

3

oligarchy, as did revolutionary England. Any proposals made, therefore, will have to appeal to Catholic theory, Catholic as to time and place, and the proposers will have to show that they are not introducing new principles but only new developments and new applications, and that their proposals are not, like those of politicians, designs to make the foreigner pay or to ride roughshod over him, or in any way to refuse him a hearing and a voice in the ecclesiastical tribunal and policy. Otherwise we should rightly expect to hear again, in the words of Bishop Sanderson's preface to the Prayer Book, the reply of the Church : " We have rejected all such proposals, as were either of dangerous consequence (as secretly striking at some established doctrine or laudable practice of the Church of England or indeed of the whole Catholick Church of Christ), or else of no consequence at all, but utterly frivolous and vain."

It ought not to need to be said, but yet it must be repeated, that no man has a right to speak of the Church at all, who does not know that he is speaking of a Great Club, formed by the Incarnate Word, during His visible sojourn with us ; that this Club is called in the New Testament the kingdom of heaven ; that it is not the narrow and uncertain little knot of " all who love the Lord Jesus Christ," but the broad and well-marked union of those whom He has loved enough to ear-mark for His sheep. Personally, if I do not belong to the Club, and the same Club, as the Apostles, I do not wish to belong to any other or newer Club. I must revert to the anarchy in which man is born, or since that is found so unsatisfying I must make a little Society of my own, which is found usually to be the same thing thinly disguised : " I am nae so sure o' John."

4

The Church of England

Starting forth with the premises, that Christ founded a Church, that the Church is the company of the baptized, and that the same is continuous and unbroken, we are first encountered by the sophism that this Church is invisible, "a creature of fire and dew," says one writer, meaning rather of moonshine and mist. It is intangible and indeterminate. Only the cock-sure and the blatant egoist can be certain that he belongs to it, and even he cannot assure us that he will be there to-morrow or five minutes hence. "It is built not upon a form and ceremony, but upon the human heart," a treacherous foundation. It apparently must not intrude upon the visible world or tithe the visible pig. It must not have chapels or tea-meetings, or political propaganda. Its ministers "must wear no clothes to distinguish them from their Christian brethren." It must not live at Peckham or Hampstead. In fact it must avoid the Aristotelian logic and all contact with the life of man, which is both visible and invisible. Opponents of this calibre need not detain any man for long. They are self-convicted of superstition and contradiction, whenever they build conventicles or meet for mummery. Their tenets can be left to the schoolmaster and the *lion comique*, who will help them to learn and to laugh.

But a far more reasonable and dangerous opposition arises from the people who admit the premises to be historically and logically correct and then add that Churches indeed are visible, but where is the Church ? Are we to take Christendom as one, when it is so obviously at sixes and sevens ? When large sections denounce and upbraid other sections ? When those who claim to represent the largest sections proclaim the rest as disqualified and de-

God's Co-operative Society

Christianised, cut off from the Universal Church and comparable only to heathen ?

Alas ! no one denies the facts. Actually the Church is like gunpowder where the charcoal, nitre, and sulphur are partly separated, each section being charged with an excess of one ingredient. The use of each is impaired. The velocity of the missile is lowered, and artillery served with these inferior explosives gets outclassed. Each section loses power for the want of the others. The dangers we are in because of our unhappy divisions are the dangers of outward defeat because of inward loss, the loss of exactly those qualities which are needed to win our share of the field. Meantime we only aggravate the evil by pride and exaggeration. No one has all the charcoal, all the nitre, or all the sulphur. None has the proportion it means to have and boasts of having. The reunion of Christendom is the first step towards effective campaigning ; but that step will only be taken if we are alive to its importance and resolutely in earnest for it to be taken. No other conception of the Church than that of one Church may ever be entertained ; indeed any other is heresy, and as such ruled out by the very terms of Churchmanship and of prayer, in every Catholic communion. But while we admit, with shame and horror, the evil plight of Christendom, we must be careful not to exaggerate it. Upon how much are we agreed ? Upon how little, proportionally, are we thus evilly divided ? We are at one, almost, upon expressed doctrine, on the necessity of the Gospel Sacraments, valid orders, absolution, the terms of Church membership, the story of the Word made flesh, and the description of the Church. Even in matters of discipline we are less divided than many seem to know.

6

The Church of England

As the Way, the Truth, and the Life are all one, yet we can point to no man, and no group of men, who tread the way unerringly, hold the whole truth, and live the complete life, so it is with the Church. The ideal remains, informs and gives power to the actual, although the actual never once expresses the ideal and always depresses it. The only way towards unity is, intellectually speaking, to perceive it, to assume it, and to set our minds against everything that hinders it.

But, says the opponent, is not this to undo the work of the Reformation ? How can there be a national Church at all, if the supernational one is of such supreme importance ? Are we to saw off the branch upon which we sit ?

One of the many noble dicta of the late T. H. Green was that the secret of right thought is to unite without unifying and to distinguish without dividing. This is the English plea in religion. It is the complete summary of the true *via media*, which is not a timid causeway between two streams or two sewers, but an isthmus uniting two continents. The pre-Reformation Church united and unified, the post-Reformation sects distinguish and divide. The question which came up for settlement at the Reformation was answered in England, and in England alone, in a way which gives the Church a commanding military position. That answer was the sane English one of constitutional government, and consequently of room for the nation within the supra-national union.

Before considering the work of the Reformation, it is certainly well to ask this pertinent question : What was the teaching of the Founder of the Church and of His earlier interpreters of the Faith upon the subject of the nation ? He was born a Jew, circumcised and admitted into the

7

fellowship of the severest nation and the most national religion. He upheld the traditions and remained strictly within the borders of the nation. He was not sent in visible presence, save to the lost sheep of the House of Israel. The manifold message He bequeathed came to all nations in their own tongues. The God, who gave us each a personality, a family, and a nation, according to Christian theory, gave us also a Society in which all nations became one. The drag-net of the Gospel, as Origen points out, gathers the Gentiles from every race ; but it leaves them their racial characters. The laudable zeal of Christian politicians, on behalf of unity certainly, in the ages of feudal reconstruction, pressed into unification that part of Christendom which it was able to coax or to coerce. Without unduly or idolatrously exalting the nation, we may ask that it should find a place, though only a subordinate place, in the Catholic economy. We ask this because the nation is not of man's making, like his systems of political government, but of God's gift ; because the archangels themselves are the spirits of nations—St. Michael, the aggressive spirit of the Church, being not the only, though the chief of these great spirits. We ask it, because the very principle of distinguishing without dividing and uniting without unifying is the secret of man's body in health, of his saner polity, and even of the holy, blessed, and glorious Trinity, upon Whom all things depend, and in whose image we all are made, remade, and inspired.

A just and reasoned demand certainly implies a just and reasoned concession to the principles appealed to. It must be admitted that we have been exceedingly slow to grant to others what we challenge for ourselves. " The Church of England and Ireland " is still the official title of the Australian Catholics, and in many ways our own house requires to be put in order, before we can make an honest and effective appeal to the rest of the Christian world. The pessimist poet begged for ruth because he

> " Could not always see the very truth,
>   And did not always sing the truth he sees ;
>   But something pleasanter to foolish ears,
>   Which should be tickled not by straws, but spears."

Let us admit our gross mistakes quite candidly, without attempting either to use against others or to admit against ourselves the argument from abuse, which Coleridge, with splendid disdain, declared not only no Christian man, but no honest man, would ever use.

With these preliminaries, we can now examine the question : Would you undo the work of the Reformation ?

What was the work of the Reformation ? The question is a complex one. The disruptions, civil wars, heresies and massacres, the breaking of the social ladders, the furies, the destruction of charities and benefit societies, these and many other unhappy things were the actual work of the Reformation. One set of writers will tell us that the work of the Reformation was the English Bible, Shakespeare, the whole splendour and glory of the later England. Another will say that the work of the Reformation was an outburst of cruelty and filthiness, the refounding of a sham Church by a lewd king, the destruction of nearly all that was lovely and tender and gracious in human worship and human life, the kindling of a fire that was one day to burn up all that was just and ordered in Church and State. Many writers exalt the actors on one side into heroes and depress their opponents into infamy. A

9

judicious modern historian thinks that men on all sides
were so base, that it is dangerous for a young man to
study the period, lest he learn cynicism and defilement.
The whoops of anarchists, unbelievers, and whim-wor-
shippers are mingled with the groans and howls of un-
taught and indignant Catholics. Both parties mean the
results rather than the work of the Reformation. Its
results cannot be undone ; but if by the work, we mean
the aim and general purpose of the movement, then this
requires to be stated and briefly summed up, and the
answer to the question will be self-evident.

But before attempting this hazardous task, it is but fair
to say that in the mouth of an English questioner, the
Reformation means the Reformation not in Germany or
Switzerland, not even in Scotland or Holland, but in
England. Whether Germans ought to wear sackcloth,
because of the work of their Reformation, may be left
an open question. It does not concern us. Probably
they ought to undo it with all their national thoroughness
and the delicate spiritual insight for which they are so
conspicuous. Possibly they ought to return to it,
as to something better than they have got at present.
Anyhow, on principle, it is not our business. We have no
Boniface and no Alcuin to spare in these dark ages. But
we ourselves have to bear the sins of our fathers, where
they went astray, and we can claim and enjoy the mercy
upon thousands, where they did right.

The Reformation in England extends from the year 1531,
when the Church of England asserted the royal supremacy,
to the settlement of 1662, when the last revision of the
Prayer Book was completed. It was neither wholly blessed
and glorious, as some people assert ; nor wholly lamentable

The Church of England

and abominable, as others say. In fact, there is no one adjective that can describe it, or its agents. Our object must not be to praise it, or to blame it, before we first try to understand it. This is less exciting, but more salutary, than the usual method of coining hot phrases and epigrams.

When all that is irrelevant and misleading has been cut away, and when all the (immoral) arguments from abuse have been dismissed, there remains this central fact that whole nations, our own among them, came to the conclusion that the powers assigned to the Pope by Canon Law had grown too great for the peace and welfare of Christendom, and that those powers ought to be curtailed. If this conclusion was fundamentally right, it makes no difference whether those who supported it were saints or scoundrels. Nor does the personal character of the Pontiff make a bad case good or a good one bad. There are some powers which even saints might not wield with safety to themselves and others, and among these are the powers of lordship which the Gentiles exercise, against which our Lord Himself warned the greatest of His saints.

Now from the Conquest onward, for five centuries the Popes had accumulated and wielded very great powers indeed, and by no means wielded them unrighteously throughout ; but they certainly had claims and enforced them often enough, which claims would have greatly astonished St. Gregory Magnus. When Cranmer was at Cambridge he made a collection of some of these. They assert, among other things, that :

1. If any man denies that the Pope is ordained of God to be primate of all the world, he is an heretic, and cannot be saved.

2. Princes' laws have no force against the Pope's decrees.

3. To oppose those decrees is to sin against the Holy Ghost.

4. These are of obligation upon laymen, as well as upon clergymen.

5. The Pope may depose kings and release subjects from oaths of obedience.

6. He may annul sentences in temporal causes.

7. Nothing may be done against one who appeals to him.

8. He may use force against anybody.

9. He is above all Councils.

In other words, the canonical position of the Pope before the Reformation was king of kings and lord of lords, in the most worldly sense. He was not only autocrat of the Church and of the world, but he superseded all conciliar and synodical government in the Church, and, by so doing, had become, theoretically, the one bond of union, the feudal overlord of every man and every State. The foremost ecclesiastical lawyer in England, William Lyndwood, wrote in 1430 a book called the *Provinciale*. He had ample means of knowing both the theory and the practice of the Canon Law, and he speaks of the three collections of decretals that were issued by Gregory IX, Boniface VIII, and John XXII, by which this tremendous power was asserted and codified, as not only accepted in theory by English Churchmen, but as in active and extant use. The humbler students of history used to rest on a report of the Ecclesiastical Courts Commission (1883), and believed that the Canon Law of Rome, though always of great authority, was not held to be binding on English courts, and that even Bulls were not of force in England unless they were accepted and enforced by formal ratification by

The Church of England

Provincial and National Assemblies. But further examination shows that this never was the case either in practice or in theory; that Popes were believed to be above the law, and their decretals as good as the canons of the greatest Councils. A decretal is a law passed by a Pope without even the formal advice of the College of Cardinals.[1] We can learn from Lyndwood that there were no liberties of the Anglican Church against the papal lawgiver, and, theoretically, none for the English State. The Church, as such, had never set herself against any of these powers. The Pope exasperated English people by reservations, collations, and provisions, as they were called, by which English benefices were handed over to non-resident Italians, or even to minors and to laymen. The State took energetic action on these questions, as we all know, and passed Statutes of Provisors and Præmunire, and the like. But what kings like Edward III could do and did do, the English Church could not do and did not do. All the worst excesses of nepotic Popes were executed by English bishops and English laymen, at his command. Archbishops Langton and Peckham, and Grosseteste, it is true, had opposed Popes and appealed to Councils; but the great facts remain that up to the Reformation, the Canon Law made the Pope an almost limitless despot, and the Church in England had never claimed to modify that theory, but had accepted it, theoretically and actually.[2]

Before we ask ourselves the question, whether this entire vassalage on the one side, and this uncontrolled imperiousness on the other, which had gradually grown to such

[1] Which advice would make it a decretum.
[2] For further development of this thesis *vide* Prof. Maitland's *Roman Canon Law in the Church of England*.

extremes, were right in themselves, and whether they reflect the rule of Him whose kingdom was not of this world, it is well to face the theory, when applied to practice. There are two historical peeps which we ought to take ; two questions we may fairly ask : (1) How did the papal theory work in England before it was so vigorously opposed by the State ? and (2) How was it working in Scotland, where it was accepted by the State ? Both of these questions were rather prominent in the minds of sincere and logical persons in the sixteenth century.

I. In the year 1216, little Henry III, aged nine, came to a crown ceded to the Pope. England was for a time ruled over by papal legates. Stephen Langton, our Archbishop, the great adviser of Magna Charta, was suspended, and not allowed to return to England, even when he had submitted to the papal authority. Gualo, the legate, ruled England. He first worked for peace. He excommunicated the invading King of France ; he confirmed Magna Charta by the Council of Bristol, and this seems very promising. Alas ! it was only the promising action of a man who has stolen his neighbour's chickens, who fences them from foxes, and feeds them with maize, only to consume them at his leisure. Every month letters poured into England from Honorius III to every kind of official, from William Marshall, Earl of Pembroke, to small barons and archdeacons. The appointments are filled by papal nominees, often very bad ones. Englishmen who spoke disrespectfully to or of the legate were clapt into gaol. A fine inquisition was held about clerks who sympathised with the barons, and thus many benefices were conveniently voided. Suspect persons could always persuade the Court by fees, *e.g.* good Hugh Wallys had to ransom his Lincoln bishopric for 1100 marks, and Gualo invited presents, and frowned on all who did not bring them ; and departed well laden with spoil. His successor, Pandulf, over-rode all kingly orders and charters, appointed to all places, forbade fortifications at Marlborough, refused to allow the Chancellor to resign, forbade the King to give money to his mother, and, in a word, provoked a furious anti-papal movement, and caused a league to be formed to expel foreigners. This was over-ridden, and again we had demands such as that no man was to be preferred to any English benefice (1240) until 300 Italian clerks were provided for, and that one-fifth of all the goods of priests should be paid to the Pope to help him in his wars. The result was, in the end, civil war and universal misery, which smouldered on long after Henry III died.[1]

II. The papal autocracy had free play in Scotland, for Scotland was always used, and used herself, as England's dangerous neighbour. The more the State in England resisted papal claims, the more Scotland became the beloved daughter of Rome. The Pope was the centre of her ecclesiastical system. A system of paying tithes to great abbeys and cathedrals, instead of to parish priests, was instituted, and because the benefices were too poor to be worth preying upon individually, they were thus further impoverished. The abbeys and bishoprics were seized upon, as provision for young princes and nobles, or for the bastards of kings and great men—soldiers, children, scandalous livers were the leaders, starved and ungoverned clerks the followers. James V's five bastard sons held high Church offices, and the Pope took pay and tolerated it all. The result in this case was that the

---

[1] *History of English Church*, c. xii. W. R. W. Stevens.

God's Co-operative Society

Church was wiped out altogether, and with blood and brutality and ferocious persecution all the terrors and insolence of Calvinism were imposed upon the people. The Society which Christ founded was broken to pieces, and a new Society, founded upon rebellion and murder, with new creeds, new rules, new ministers, and, alas! with no new crimes and cruelties, took the place of that fallen Church, and there was no Reformation, but only, as Laud called it, a Deformation—a deformation of the whole Christian religion.

With these considerations, and this evidence before our eyes, we cannot possibly use the language with which some indulge themselves. The Reformation becomes a grim necessity to us, if we are anything short of ardent Vaticanists. We may deplore it, and ought to do so. We may have the greatest contempt for many who were prominent in the movement. The scoundrelism of the Reformers, the foolish and disastrous way in which the movement was exploited for political and personal ends, we may admit to the full. We may feel kindly and reverently towards the Pope, and look upon him (as I hope we do), as a great Christian Bishop, as the natural primate and Chairman of Christendom. We may and do respect the man, and pray for the Bishop : but we cannot possibly pretend that his canonical claims of dominance are to be admitted.

If the Reformation was a necessity, it was surely better that it should come after the revival of letters, when men were inspired by a new passion, and furnished with a new power, for studying the past. If it had taken place in the precocious thirteenth century, or the less intelligent fourteenth or fifteenth centuries, it would hardly have

been permanent. The English Reformers had the printer
to inform them. If the movement had been left unbegun
till the seventeenth century, it would possibly have de-
molished the doctrine of the Apostolic Succession and the
Sacrament of Holy Orders, and so the reality and validity
of the Mass itself. If it had been put off till the eighteenth,
it would have landed us in dulness and Deism, at least with
a Dr. Johnson Prayer Book. In the nineteenth, we should
have had some silly sentimental Calvinism of a Free Church
Catechism sort, if indeed anything Christian, even in outward show and seeming, could have survived the furies
of a volcano so long choked down, and of abuses so long
bolstered up. Therefore, incidentally, we cannot but be
glad that the work had to be done by the generations who
undertook it, rather than by those who would have probably been too weak or too violent for the work. When
all is said that can be truly said, about the scoundrelism
of the Reformers (the phrase is Dr. Littledale's), it remains
a solid fact that when the work was over in 1662 we had
left us a Catholic Liturgy, the full deposit of the Faith, an
unbroken succession, and nothing in all our formulæ which
comes from heretical Luther or heretical Calvin which is
not also in the teaching of the eight great doctors of the
undivided Church. It is especially worthy of present
notice that even the second Prayer Book of Edward VI
was so careful about the deposit of Faith that it ordered
the Athanasian Creed to be recited seven more times than
did the first Prayer Book, a fact which the admirers of
that evil time would do well to note.

The pressing need of reform in Canon Law, and the fact
that Popes could hardly be expected to reform it, and
abdicate their real and imaginary thrones, caused a dead-

lock and a divided allegiance in holy souls. Not only did
the young men—the Oxford reformers of 1498—express
desires for such reform, and these included More, Fisher,
Colet, and Wareham, but the next wave of men also,
Wolsey, Stephen Gardiner, Cranmer, and nearly all other
men agreed in the fact that the strain was intolerable.
The divorce matter was not the cause of the Reformation
(or surely the movement would have been lopped off with
Queen Anne's head). It was only the occasion—an ugly
occasion enough, no doubt. But to be fair, even about
that, we must remember that the Popes had long been
very lax about such matters. Philip Augustus of France
was divorced contrary to the Pope's directions, and re-
married, and the marriage was easily allowed. Louis XII
was allowed to divorce a wife without issue. The laws of
many Church Councils on Marriage were over-ridden by
Julius II, when he dispensed Henry, and allowed him to
wed his deceased brother's wife. There was no piety, but
only policy, in Clement's refusal to undo the questionable
knot—a double policy, for he was under the thumb of
Katharine's nephew, and the lawyers were reminding him
that he would transgress a far more serious thing than
Mosaic and Church law, that was Papal law. Henry,
naturally perhaps, was amenable to no such reason, and
England, almost to a man, seemed pleased to see Canon
Law curtailed, although public opinion was genuinely
shocked by the marriage with Anne. Men left the churches
when she was prayed for as queen. But the repudiation
of papal despotic claims was accepted by the spirituality
and welcomed by the laity with overwhelming accord.
English kings had often before checked the demands of
Popes, from the Conqueror downward. The Canon Law

wiped out nations, and surely God has given us some distinctness of nationality (so they reasoned), and the king is the man to assert the same? Henry assured them that when he was called " on earth supreme head of the Church of England " (January 15, 1535), he obtained no single new power by that title ; and, civilly, he was right. But the Church and nation which thought the Reformation was now done, found that they had only exchanged one autocrat for another, that the principle of despotism was even stronger than ever, and that the constitutional reconstruction of the Government by Councils was as far from Henry's mind as it was from that of the Popes themselves. The orgies of tyranny, the hypocrisy, demoralisation, and misery that followed, may be read, faithfully recorded by Dr. James Gairdner in his *English Church in the Sixteenth Century*. The assault upon the monasteries, the destruction of the educational and social ladders, the rebellions, the change to landlordism, the unbelief, despair, treason, reaction, and confusion, would be enough to disgust anybody with the Reformation, as a whole, if he were not aware of its grim necessity. The statutory reform of Canon Law, often mooted, was long delayed, until it was finally shelved by an Act, 1544, which re-enacted all that was not repealed by statute law. But we must always remember that there are thus very few omissions left to be prohibitions. Of course, it was not all darkness and horror. The exquisite melodies of the English Prayer Books, and their superb translations, opened new windows to many pious persons. The mediæval habit of communicating once a year gave way to better things ; but, on the whole, the outlook for true religion seemed very dark. It was darker still in Edward VI's reign, with its pillage and imposture, its intrigues and rebellions, and its ruthless, stupid cruelty to the poor. It is greatly wonderful that the Marian reaction was not far more ferocious and intense, with a far larger butcher's bill than 277 persons. But there are two important matters about this reign. First, that the three charges brought against Ridley and Latimer were : (1) They opposed the view that Christ's natural body and blood are present in the Sacrament. Cardinal Pole explained this word natural to mean sensually present. In this he was heretical and they Catholic. (2) They asserted that the *substance* of bread and wine remained after consecration, and, in their sense of the words, many orthodox theologians maintained the same, even after Transubstantiation was decreed in 1215. (3) They denied that the Mass was a propitiatory sacrifice to the non-contrite. The Council of Trent, only six years after, proclaimed that the Mass is truly propitiatory, if we draw nigh to God contrite and penitent. We must not let the folly and ignorance of modern Protestants blind us to the fact that these two men were, in many respects, at least as Catholic as their opponents and would probably themselves have burnt their modern admirers with the greatest alacrity.

The second important thing to remember in the Marian reaction, is that English Orders were certainly recognised by the Pope Paul IV, who declared in 1555 that those who "have been restored to unity we will indulgently receive in their orders and benefices." How this can be reconciled with *Apostolicæ Curæ* we must leave our Roman friends to explain.[1]

Neither the shocks and cabals of the foreign Protestants,

[1] *Leo XIII versus Paul IV.* Parker. London, 1898.

nor the gentle wooing of Pius IV, who, in 1561, offered to recognise the English Prayer Book; neither the Spanish invasion, the plots, the excommunications, nor the frantic attempts made to join us with Lutherans and Calvinists, shook the Church of England from her perfectly sound and fundamental conclusion, that though the Canon Law was intolerable in many respects, the Catholic Society did not depend upon any of its abuses, and was competent to reform it. Queen Elizabeth, in 1570, issued a *Declaration of the Queen's Proceedings*, and said that she had no power or claim to define the Faith or change the ceremonial from " the form before received and observed by the Catholic and Apostolic Church," but she did claim " the duty of a Christian prince to see that her subjects lived in the faith and obedience of Christian religion, that the ecclesiastical government be duly carried on, and that no further inquisition is made as regards faith, so long as people profess the Christian Faith defined by the Holy Scripture and the Creeds, nor as regards ceremonies and externals, so long as the people are outwardly conformable. As to papal claims to over-ride and supersede this authority, when the occasion offers of an impartial, free, and general assembly of Christendom, such an answer shall be made as will prove satisfactory."

The enormous power of the Crown, strengthened by this limitation of Canon Law, had itself to be limited on its political side; and limited by an impartial, free, and general assembly of Englishmen called Parliament. It was limited —not, as we know, without great convulsions, and certainly not by such a Parliament, but by a partial and tyrannous body of rich merchants and capitalists. The new powers of the commercial classes gave rise to all sorts of sects, who have pared the everlasting gospel to suit commercial aims and commercial morality. The Church was penalised, attacked, suppressed, persecuted, but at no time did she falter or turn out of her path, and the divines of the Restoration refused any compromise with despotic Popes or anarchic Calvinists, and left us still the power to say, that to a real Œcumenical Council—to an impartial, free, and general assembly of Christendom—such answer shall be made as will prove satisfactory. But we must remember that all our doings, our care for the Faith, and for all that sets it forth, must be such as bear out that solemn, reasonable, and impassioned appeal.

From what has been set forth in the above sketch, it will be easily seen that there is one man in England who is bound, so long as Roman Canon Law remains what it is, to embody one official protest against it, and that man is our Sovereign and Representative, whose office is wrongfully hindered by the laws and decrees, which are incompatible with our life as a nation. When he assumes, not his regenerate life, but his royal office, and once in his life and on one point, he is logically bound to protest against papal claims, and he does so. Personally, I see no cause for dismay in this sole use of the term Protestant, which, used without high and sufficient cause, is unmerciful and disgraceful in the deepest degree. St. Bernard wrote to Eugenius III: " Bethink thee before all things that the holy Roman Church, over which, by God's doing, thou dost preside, is the Mother of Churches, and not the mistress, that thou art not the lord of bishops, but one amongst them, nay, rather, a brother of God's lovers and a comrade of them who fear Him" (*De Consideratione*, Lib. IV., c. vii.). Is that an uncatholic speech, or a novelty,

The Church of England

or uncharitable, or heretical ? If it is none of these things, then do not let us be frightened because our people have said the same, nor confuse our real standpoint with those of the cheap religions made in Germany, Holland, and Switzerland, for ours was made in Heaven.

" We are personally much beholden to the Pope," said James I in 1604, " but his claim to dispose of kingdoms and dispense subjects from their obedience is subversive of all government, and there will be no security till a general Council has declared against it." [1]

But while the Church sounded this consistent note, she resisted the attempts of the disloyal Low Churchmen to rob her of her faith, her continuity, and her Catholic name and heritage. An evil crew of foreigners and heretical Englishmen tried to rush the defences in the early years of Elizabeth, and of these Bucer (the gentleman who wished to give us polygamy as a gospel privilege) is the most favourable specimen. The violence, disloyalty and insolence of the Puritans ought to be better understood than it is. They formed constant cabals against the Prayer Book and the whole direction and government of the Church, eating her bread and mocking at her doctrines. They chose their own services and loudly proclaimed their hatred of everything historic, lovely and Catholic. They tried by cajolery and violence to bring the English Church to the absolutely fatal position of Continental Protestants, who snapped the continuity of the Divine Society, introduced new doctrines, and refashioned everything in a lordly security that all they did was founded upon Scrip-

[1] *History of the English Church, Elizabeth and James I.* By W. H. Frere.

ture, and Scripture was founded upon—nothing. Here are their boastful confessions :

1. The Swiss : The Scriptures have authority sufficient of themselves, not of men.

2. The Belgic : We take the Scriptures not because the Church accepts them, but because the Holy Ghost testifies to our consciences that they came from God.

3. The Wittenburg (Augustana) has the same thing, only slightly more veiled, when it defines the Church as those who agree in the pure and wholesome doctrine of the gospel, and asserts that to agree with that doctrine is unity enough. (So the Scotch Art. XIX.)

Is it not remarkable and instructive that these three places, Germany, Belgium, and Switzerland, where the Bible was exalted above the Church, should now be the centres of a furious and bitter destructive school of criticism ? [1] Is it not still more remarkable that in spite of all the assaults by arms, argument and abuse, made upon her by the Papal party, the Church of England refused to have anything to do with these as allies, although the adherents of the Westminster Confession managed for a time to get entire dominance in the State (see their Art. I and IV), and, presuming that biblical authority does not depend upon the Church, worked for the total prohibition of every single office of the Prayer Book. In secure and confident defiance of all who think that the Church's one foundation is Jonah and the whale, and of all who think that it is personal and private inspiration, she gave us the

---

[1] The Bible is torn in pieces and Jesus Christ is blasphemed from Leyden to Berlin and from Berlin to Basle by theologians and professors who call themselves Protestants, but are the allies of infidelity. —*L. Pullan.*

The Church of England

true and ripe results of all the blood, blunders, battles, and confusion of the Reformation in the settlement of 1662. The Reformation settlement is our present Prayer Book, ornaments rubric and all. Of this we may say with Dr. Gairdner, " No formularies were ever drawn that give so much liberty to the human mind," and " they constitute a more real Catholicism than that of the Council of Trent."

At the present crisis, when popular clamour demands a reconstruction of our war-worn defences, won and held with such faith, such valour and such heroism, when the old ramparts are being assailed again from without, and when, alas! some are foolish and base enough to advocate surrender, modification, and reconstruction from within, it is well to remind ourselves that we are the sons and successors of men who dared to be entirely Catholic and yet set bounds to despotism, who valued liberty so much that they repudiated both individualism and unreason.

To wish to undo the work of the Reformation is therefore not only absurd, but even criminal. It is *lese majesté* against every nation under heaven. It is to affirm a principle which tears off some of the limbs of the Church and crushes others into a shapeless pulp. It is to make the Church always weakest where the nation is strongest and as such needs her most, and vice versa. Finally, it is to precipitate a conflict between honest patriotism and the Catholic Faith, which is not only unwise, but actually irreligious. The Church in England is rightly entitled the Church of England, because she has reformed the Canon Law to prevent the suppression of the nation.

CHAPTER II

ENGLISH AND OTHER CATHOLICS

FROM the foregoing view of the Reformation and the English Church, it will be seen that the real divergence of opinion between the daughter and her Roman mother, with the rest of the Western family, is narrow but clear and deep and well defined. The first process of healing wounds, in ecclesiastical as well as in medical science, is obviously to clear the wound, not only of irritating prejudices but of jagged edges. That seems to be one of the duties of English Churchmen. Indeed we are in effect called to that office by the very powers and position which we possess; by the assured vantage-ground which our fathers took up; by the aloofness and detachment of our island quarters; by the good temper and coolness which we have been obliged to cultivate in dealing with many races; by the sense of fair play which we try to adopt and often fancy that we have attained because we desire to attain it. But because there is a certain principle for which we must contend with the greatest earnestness, that is no reason at all why we should add a great many more vexed questions to that quarrel, merely to gain sophistical or academic victories or to weaken an adversary, whom we have no right and should have no desire to weaken at all. The customs of worship which are not our customs are, on our own principle, to be left to the nations which admit them to accept or to criticise. The exact amount of worship to be paid in public to the Mother of God and to the Saints, the use of the Blessed Sacrament of the Altar for benediction and reverence apart from Communion ; whether discipline is best served by celibate or (permissively) married priests ; whether Confession should be enforced in public and allowed in private, as with us, or whether it should be compulsory in private, as with the Latin Communion ; all these things and many more are matters which we should tolerate in others, and perhaps ask whether they might not be useful to correct our own obvious shortcomings, our coldness, pride, self-indulgence, and hatred of discipline. If we discuss them at all, it will be as matters which are all beside the true point of that division, which we deeply deplore but for which we cannot accept full responsibility.

Because we are one, we shall always be careful not to worship before altars which are set up in opposition to the Catholic altar, whether in this country or any other. If in France we may not communicate with French Catholics, we shall join devoutly in their worship, as far as we may. In England where we find altar set up against altar, we shall be scrupulous not to attend Roman places of worship. At the same time we shall remind ourselves that not only in the Mass, in the prayer for the Church Militant, but in Matins, Evensong, and the Litany we always pray for the Pope, among the bishops of the Church, and that we owe to him not only the forms of faith which we possess, a very large part of our prayers, worship and ritual, but almost the whole of our Church organisation. We can constantly remember that Almighty God has not sent us into the world to make up a religion out of our inner conscience, or to compound one by selection. Just as there are certain elemental arrangements which are His gift, so there are ministrations to these which are His further gift. A man when he comes into life does not drop here like an isolated thunderbolt. He has not only his peculiar and private life and outlook, but he is part of a family. That family is part of a tribe or shire, the tribe part of the nation, the nation part of a group division, and the division part of the great human stock. We find these things : we do not make them. They are not the creatures of Christian or civilised society. They are God's will and construction. If we ask why He willed them, it seems a sufficient reason to say that they are the stairs or rungs by which men climb from the isolated animal life of the selfish and separate creature to the catholic and spiritual life of perfect love and mercy. The self is a starting-point ; the family to enlarge the self ; the tribe to keep the family from becoming hard and exclusive ; the nation to enlarge the petty bounds of the tribe ; the colour and other divisions to overleap the bounds of the nation ; and the common human nature above all and through all and in us all, which is the very portal to God. The friend of man who is his mother's enemy, his people's enemy, his country's enemy, or the white man's enemy is obviously so much less the friend of man.

Now when the new life came to us in Christ, did it contradict or did it sanction this existing order ? Plainly the latter. The Word not only became man, but became the man Christ Jesus, taking a human personality to devote in continuous sacrifice. He was in subjection to a family. He was the lion of His tribe. He was emphatically of His nation. He followed the national organisation of twelve

English and Other Catholics

tribes in His twelve apostles. Yet He was not for that nation only. He was not the second Abraham but the second Adam. Each bond was admitted and transcended. The perfect life distinguished but did not divide, united but did not unify.

The Church proceeds exactly on these lines. She sealed individuality by the new name in Baptism. She found and blessed the family. She found and recognised the tribe and nation. At Pentecost it would have been just as easy to endow hearers with understanding as to give gifts of divers languages, but (*pace* Bede) each man heard not Latin, Greek, or Aramaic, but the tongue in which he was born. As the Church spread she spread over political divisions, largely in and by the Roman peace. Her dioceses were given political borders, her synods convened from pre-arranged areas. Christendom itself was roughly coterminous with the empire. Rome, as the head city, became early of great ecclesiastical importance. If St. Peter was the chief apostle (and we think he was), if he was Bishop of Rome (and we hold it to be so), he was called to that see because it was the chief one, not to make it so. This was asserted to be the position of Rome by two General Councils, that of Constantinople in 381 and of Calcedon in 451.[1]

Not only by her choice of sees and sites did the Church set her seal upon national and tribal existence. She did so by her explicit teaching. The very word piety which she adopted meant duty to family and nation. "To observe the customs of one's fathers, so far as they are good and holy," was enjoined not only by the Clementine homilies (c. viii.), but by the constant and perpetual com-

---

[1] It is fair to remember that St. Leo protested against this decision.

mands to civil obedience which came in an unbroken succession from the Apostles onwards. These were rightly and strongly appealed to by all the apologists, and the principle is to be found in all patristic teaching, taking definite form in the words St. Augustine quotes (*Ep. ad Casul et passim*), that "in those things concerning which divine scripture does not speak with certainty the custom of our ancestors is to be held as law." With those people who are a law and a religion to themselves, who take the anarchist standpoint, we are not at present concerned. But the citizens of the heavenly kingdom, the Church, may and must grant that She has approved of the natural organisms of man. They are of the Father; but the kingdom of the Son surely transcended all these in a mighty and motherly pre-eminence? The Church must be both of and above the nation? That too must be granted. The English Church has never claimed to be above the decrees of the whole Church, nor has even the State as yet presumed so far, although it has cast off its allegiance and may provoke a desperate conflict at any time. The toast is still Church and King, not King and Church. The Church has always appealed to the Œcumenical Councils of the past and of the future, which shall represent not the Latin interest or the English, Greek, or Armenian interest, but the interest of Christ's marked sheep. The Catholic Church is above the English Church, as England is above Yorkshire, as Somerset is above one of its villages, as any village is above one family in it, as that family is above one of its members. No more and no less. In all these the right relation is confessed daily and hourly. My family claim my loyalty, but they may not rob or imprison me. The just parish does not ignore its poorest household.

English and Other Catholics

England does not count the love of county to be treasonable, but fosters it in ships and regiments. The Church of England is united in dioceses under a primate, who is not headmaster or sovereign but chairman of bishops. The whole Church we should expect to be of national Churches distinguished but not divided. We see nothing of the kind. Christendom resembles Europe under Napoleon. One country was then, one Church in the West is now unobliterated. In the hatred, fear, passion and unreason of conflict, blows fall on innocent victims. The air is full of lies, which pretend to be history. One party cries up Smithfield and forgets Tyburn, penal laws are passed over and Guy Fawkes remembered, or the Armada is sunk out of sight and the Irish massacres thrown upon the screen. A man who wishes to be both honest and charitable and not to be found beating his fellow-servants, gets to lose sight of the just cause of quarrel, in the perplexity of abuses on all sides. The humble and the contrite heart must belong to nations, as well as to persons, and we have much to repent of in our past.

Perhaps we can go so far as to say that the domination and autocracy of the mediæval Popes served a great purpose, in earlier times. It kept us from insularity. If itself it was pagan and even insolent, it bitted and bridled the equally pagan and insolent power of barons and kings. If it was often abused, it was often used for freedom and holiness. If it was not the noblest bond, at least it was a centripetal force. If it did not unite East and West, at least it united the West. Since English Catholics have need of Spanish ones and of all others, the Pope gave us some of these ; and the more grateful we are for what we once had, the more we deplore the element which lost us

so many of our fellow-Christians. Could we ever else have
hounded on the heathen against Christian Russia or have
rejoiced to see Catholic France under the iron feet of non-
Catholic Germany? should we ever have fallen into the
confusion and ruin of religion at home, into desolating
Protestant schisms, if the nexus of Unity had been gentle
and measured instead of harsh and overbearing? Would
the Arts have perished and the daughters of Music been
laid so low, if the chairman of Christendom had not claimed
to rule without a Parliament? The appeal of the English
Church is now, and has been, from the one-man decision
of His Holiness the Pope, to a General Council, to be called
by the express consent, assent, and agreement not only
of the Pope, but of the residue of Christian Princes, as
the Convocation pleaded in 1536 and again in 1537, just
before the Council in Mantua.

We must here confess with shame that the perplexity
of the sixteenth-century reformers is near akin to hypocrisy. Jewel now seems to exalt and now to depress the
place of Councils, in his *Defence* and Appendix. In 1534
and again in 1559 the English Parliament actually blocked
the way of Councils by forbidding any person, religious or
other, to depart out of the king's dominions to any Council.[1]
There was no Church protest. The XXIst Article, the
Homily on Whitsuntide, and many of our greatest writers,
e.g. Jeremy Taylor,[2] speak with hesitating and uncertain
voice and warn us that even General Councils must not
be anti-scriptural. Even with the luminous and fair comments of Tract XC, there is not a great and hearty clarity
of voice, although perhaps at any time (and it is to be
hoped for all future time) most English Churchmen would

---

[1] *Stubbs' Documents*, p. 226.   [2] *Ductor*, III. c. iv, rule 21.

English and Other Catholics

agree with Hooker that " the best, the safest, and most sincere and reasonable way is the verdict of the whole Church, orderly taken and set down in the assembly of some General Council."

Meantime surely very much can be done to ensure better relations. We can all try to forget the mistakes of the past. We can all set ourselves to erect no new barriers. We can remind all our people that to call a thing Roman Catholic is no reproach ; that we do not deny the validity of Roman orders and other sacraments ; that one of the books of the New Testament was directed to Roman Catholics. The more clearly we know the real dispute, the less likely we shall be to start factitious quarrels, to find fault with prayers in other tongues, with the manners of people whom we do not know, and with worship which is too warm for our cold hearts and too prostrate for our stiff knees.

Above all things the greatest source of disunion and individualism in religion is the unreasonable and baseless view about the Bible, which is but too common among devout English people. Even in the zeal and excitement about the Divine Library which prevailed in the seventeenth century, the Second Sunday in Advent was provided with a beautiful Collect, describing the Christian use of the Scriptures. These are for learning, to teach patience, to bring the comfort of the Holy Word (which is not the Bible, but the living Christ), and to inspire hope. Faith is not mentioned. The Bible is not the rule of faith. We did not promise at our Baptism to believe the Bible. The Church is not founded upon it. It is not the one thing needful. It was written, composed, gathered, preserved, and translated by Churchmen and for Churchmen. Many

of the dead in Christ never knew there was or would be a
New Testament at all. When we have it, it is not of
private interpretation. It has quite other than the literal
meanings, as we assert when we sing the *Gloria* after each
psalm. These are often the exact opposite of the author's
meanings. The Church has the right to contradict the
Bible. For instance, in Psalm lxxxviii, verses 10, 11,
and 12, the poet expected the answer No, to his questions.
The Church gives the answer Yes, and uses the psalm as
proper for Good Friday. If abuses were ever an argument
against use, surely the misuse of the Bible would be an
overwhelming reason for denying it to nearly everybody.
The proud ignoramus, who thinks that a Bible in his knap-
sack makes him master of the highest wisdom, is in a
perilous condition indeed. He fancies that he is bound
by a golden rope to the heavenly Guide, so that no pre-
cipices need now trouble him in the slightest. He actually
believes that he has the Eternal Word in his fingers, that
the Word took print instead of flesh, that a work of human
mechanics is the Divine device for his salvation. He pits
the handmaidens, the writings of the holy servants, against
the Mother and Mistress of Christians, against the Bride
of God. He will prove to you that the Bible is inspired,
because it says, or he thinks it says, that it is inspired ;
that it cannot err, nor he err in construing it. The plenary
inspiration of the bumptious reader is the sole creed of
such unfortunate wanderers. Every man becomes in-
fallible without further ado. Let him once have an
authorised or loose version, sold under cost price, he is
fully equipped for heaven. No greater device was ever
invented for ruining the sweetness, modesty, and gradua-
tion of the soul in the School of Christ. No wonder the

ever-worshipped Bible becomes the object of the utmost contempt and derision. Often the earnest youth, trained in Bible adoration, ends as the most bitter detractor of what he ought never either to adore or to burn.

Let any man turn to the history of the British and Foreign Bible Society, written by William Canton in five volumes and published by John Murray. He will be amazed to find that so many clever, determined, practical Englishmen are hot-foot upon the dissemination of the Scriptures, as the only hope for the world. The surgery contains all the medicines known to science ; let every man have a key in his breeches pocket and he will be able to grapple with any disease which afflicts him. Once that key is in the pocket and used, suffering will be no more. Never do our beloved countrymen come out more wisely— with practical wisdom, that is—than in the work of this terrific Society. All the arts of the city, all the devices known to advertisers, are used to circulate the Bible, in all quarters and all tongues. It will purge all cholers and knit all lesions. Blacks will grow white upon it and the Balkans will blossom as the rose with amity and bene- volence. Whatever the diseases of the world, the panacea has been discovered, and Peckham shall prescribe. Show anywhere a sufferer and, by some means or other, the pill will be darted into his pylorus. The versions are made with care and scholarship. When made they are stuffed into knapsacks and shovelled into hospitals. In- scribed copies are sent after every battle to the bereaved families. Is there an explosion ? Before the victim is well on the stretcher a Testament is by his ribs. Pathans find portions in their forts, Arabs in their burnouses, sailors in bunks, and Esquimaux in igloos. Albanians can read

God's Co-operative Society

the Epistle to Timothy in Gleg and Tosk. Sentries on the Aventine get the Romans in Italian. Kurds con the Revelations in Kermanshahi, and Carlist or Portuguese rebels have less certainty of rations than of Synoptics in their own tongues. Mild surprises at the perversity of the aliens come to this great writer. The recipients do not profit by their portions. They sometimes only light pipes. Priests, who are always expected to persecute, sometimes applaud. Lutherans, who might be expected to help, mob the hawkers when they find the Apocrypha is not included ; for without Susanna and the Elders, what is life worth to Lutherans ? The pious Turk is shocked that saints are mentioned without their proper titles. Brigands rob but read ; though alas ! they rob again. The books are used as amulets, charms, prizes for "houpla." The Makalana tribe have already begun on the Thessalonians. The enthusiasts of Lourdes are approached, when they are sore with failure. The Kaiser has been lured to beam upon the effort ; and in fine 194,655,313 of the Society's publications, without counting their further efforts for the last seven years, have drenched this illiterate globe. It is hard to deal with such astute and passionate enthusiasm which is so praiseworthy and so reactionary, not excessive but exclusive overmuch, so full of praise for one of the Church's works and so derisive of the Church which works, so fond of the fruit and so rough to the tree, so idolatrous of the means and so blind to the end. In this tremendous Society we have the whole problem of English religion, its power and its limitations. Men who love education, poetry, national speech, culture and the quickening of thought, must rejoice to see that the work of this company helps forward all these matters. The one thing it does not help forward, unless it be unconsciously, is the proportion of the Faith and the clear light and true knowledge of the Son of God.

It is part of the mechanical habit of thought to which we are a prey, that we can think of bodies of thought (not only Christian but any bodies of thought) as matters which can be dealt with by simple addition and instalment. If we telegraph : " Send me a physician or a governour for a province," we do not expect, indeed we should be very surprised to have a reply, " Head forwarded by this day's mail, trunk next week, members, appurtenances, instruments, and uniform to follow later." But when we ask for the Christian Faith, or the New Theology, or anything else, we seem quite content to be told, " Here are one or two doctrines to go on with, more shall follow next century." We have carried independence to such lengths that we have forgotten that life hangs upon interdependence. Other nations have kept interdependence perhaps equally exclusively, so that they have similarly forgotten that the independence of the limbs is just as necessary to an unpalsied life as their cohesion in the body.

Is the reunion which we desire, for which Christ prayed, to be accomplished first outwardly and then in the realm of the spirit ? Would the blessed consummation take effect merely if the successor of St. Augustine renewed his filial duties to the successor of St. Gregory ? if the successor of St. Gregory again adopted a liberal and fatherly and modest attitude towards the successor of St. Augustine ? The problem evidently goes deeper. The new life must begin in the unseen womb of the soul. It must be fed by prayer and charity and nourished by a wholesomer, bolder thought, circulating in the life-blood

God's Co-operative Society

of the Church, until it is fit for the ruder airs of birth in the outer and more actual world. All things point to this conception as already accomplished. It is our part to neutralise the poisons of individualism, which may mar and destroy the hope of the future—to prepare and to expect the new trust; so that when the truth comes it shall not bewilder us, but be very welcome. That seems the peculiar mission of Churchmen of our generation.

CHAPTER III

THE CHURCH AND THE CHILDREN

SOME years ago a paper was read in Oxford criticising what passes as religious education in our elementary schools. It attracted some attention, and when it was printed in the *Commonwealth* brought down so many letters, in every mood, that the author was spurred on to reprint it. It was retailed at a penny " as a mild carminative, in the hope that a digestion disordered by a hard diet of stone and serpent may be restored to such moderate health as will make a little Gospel milk not unacceptable in the future." No reviews would notice the pamphlet. It was given no advertisements. It got up upon its own legs and ran and then flew abroad. It provoked much counter-criticism. It was met by other pamphlets, which, however, did not move quite so nimbly. Several reverend divines made it their business to confute it and are still confuting. It is, most unhappily, by no means out of date, as the author hoped it would be. It was baptized " Huppim and Muppim," after the sons of Benjamin (Gen. xlvi. 21). To know these worthies is a fair example of the knowledge which still passes muster as religious education. It is a good average example, because some educators are still to be found who boast that the infants under their hands have had a complete course of lessons in " the insects of the Old Testament." [1]   Others buy real slings and

[1] Probably leaving out the only really important insect, the worm that never dies.

39

walking-sticks from Syria to illustrate and enforce their religious lessons. These eccentricities are perplexing. Our clergy have, in their earlier years at least, studied Plato. They know that all education means so to prepare the mind that when truth comes it is welcome. They know that truth is usual and ordinary or unusual and extra-ordinary, so that this preparation must be twofold. They know the story of the Annunciation, which illustrates all of this, which shows a mind which had made the most of the old stories of Jacob and David, but could perceive a new, strange truth, face it intelligently, welcome it, and submit to it. To offer comments to such men as our clergy seems to risk over-wearying them with what is to them entirely trite. Yet in effect their eyes are blinded by Huppim. They see and approve the better things, yet they follow Muppim and the insects of the Old Testament. The very flies and lice have a hallowed buzz and a spiritual bite, when they are hatched in so august a land. Natu-rally the criticism of the teaching given by the clergy leads on to a criticism of the teaching given to the clergy. A second pamphlet came out, under the title " And Ard " (the third of Benjamin's sons). This also flew about, but it was kindly entertained by the press. It also is unfor-tunately not the least out of date. Both pamphlets con-sequently are here given *in extenso*.

HUPPIM AND MUPPIM

The New Education Acts, so pleasing to Dissenters, have one very obvious merit. The clergy are evidently to be kept trotting briskly, in a heavy set of brass Government

The Church and the Children

harness, until they tire of pulling the weight of so-called secular education. This harness will be from time to time improved with heavier bits and weightier breeching: the load will be added to, and, after a little flicking and even flogging, it will then become evident that the light-draught clerical animal is unfit for such a severe strain. He will have to be unyoked, and kept to his own particular work. Religious education will be assigned to him, as it should be, and the rest will be hauled by the great Government traction engines as well as may be.

Then, at some expense of time and temper, perhaps we shall begin to understand what religious education (in a strictly elementary sense) really is ; and we may hope that two exasperating fallacies which haunt our controversialists will then be laid to rest. These two have disfigured for a long time the schemes and speeches of our so-called educationalists.

The first is that it is " godless " to teach any honest lore even without collects, but particularly godless to teach arithmetic, pothooks, or hendecasyllables without collects before and after. Yet the gymnasium is not called godless. The drill-sergeant might, but usually does not, begin his exercises with the collect for the Second Sunday in Lent. We seem to agree that to bring the body into strength and under control is a wholesome and holy work, which fits us for the Resurrection of the body. Why can we not agree that the same is true of the intellectual powers ?— that to develop these is, so far, a holy work ; and that every step towards the perfect stature is of itself a step towards the Son of God ? There seems no reason to doubt that civil powers may do holy work ; unless, that is to say, that we are consistent anarchists, we must not attack

God's Co-operative Society

honest teaching as godless. But, if we are consistent anarchists, godless is a word with no meaning to us.

The second fallacy, which afflicts really superior persons upon the other side of the quarrel, is a certain blind belief in facts, as they call them, in detached, isolated notions, such as the number of the planets, the specific gravity of zinc, and the like. Believers in God claim that no facts, and no haystacks of facts, are of value at all, unless they are united by a true conception of Him, and thus knit together with all other facts by a strong central thought. This true conception of God fertilises every form of knowledge. For instance, arithmetic without it is a foolish study, likely to end in roguery. But then so is boot-making; so are book-writing, cooking, electrical engineering, and darning; so are all the varied trades and occupations of men and women. Yet no one seriously proposes that archdeacons should direct mines, rural deans preside at cattle markets, canons organise exhibitions of mangles, fat women, and waxworks, because all these, without thought of God, are unfruitful and sinful. But because without that great thought the grace is gone from the simplest or the most skilful work, it does not follow that the wretched clergy should spend their short tithes and times in keeping a tight grip over the shrimping trade, or insisting that apprentices at oil and butter vats gird on their aprons prayerfully. Yet, if anybody, then everybody always needs the knowledge of God, whatever his age or work may be.

If children and quite illiterate persons need this knowledge of God, quite as much as do old, intelligent, or learned folk, then it follows that this knowledge must be quite an easy one, and easily acquired. The necessary thoughts

42

The Church and the Children

about God are, and must be, few, plain, and simple, so that they may find an entrance into the minds of quite small babes and simple peasants ; may inform our first and easiest actions and dispose these in the way of everlasting life. If the foaming and fury about religious education were made by men as sincere and reasonable as they are furious, we should hear much about these few plain thoughts, these grains of mustard seed. Our religious leaders would teach them clearly and persistently, and make them known on all sides.

But the fact is otherwise. Children pass in crowds and shoals through the academies which our passionate shepherds manage and superintend. They stream forth over the world after years and years of so-called religious education ; and what have they learnt ? Let the opponents of voluntary schools give ear. These children can tell you who Huppim and Muppim and Ard were ; they know the latitude of Beersheba, Kerioth, and Beth-gamul ; they can tell you who slew a lion in a pit on a snowy day ; they have ripe views upon the identity of Nathanael and St. Bartholomew ; they can name the destructive miracles, the parables peculiar to St. Luke, and above all, they have a masterly knowledge of St. Paul's second missionary journey. They are well loaded and ballasted with chronicles of Baasha and Zimri, Methuselah, and Alexander the coppersmith. This may be valuable as historical, geographical, critical, topographical, or memorial education, but it can hardly be called religious education, except in the most dissenting and unthinking use of the term. Take any of these " religiously educated " children and ask them what one must do to make life nobler and less sordid ? How may there be an increase of grace ? They simply

43

look puzzled. Ask them how one worships, and Whom ? They are silent. Ask what one does if one falls into sin, and how one obtains the remission of sins, mentioned in the Apostles' Creed ? They have not a notion. Well, then, what are the seven deadly sins to avoid ? or the seven gifts of the Holy Ghost to pray for ? What are the means of grace ? Are any of these more urgently needed than others ? There is no reply to these questions. Dr. Clifford and all his friends from the land of Dagon need not alarm themselves. Church children know nothing more about the Divine Liturgy than if they had been bred at Westbourne Park Chapel itself. Let the Dissenter who doubts this greet any children he meets with the salutation, " The Lord be with you," and behold them stare and giggle, because they do not know the answer.

Amid all the din and smoke of the battle about religious education, one thing is evident, that the people are perishing for want of knowledge, of the simple saving knowledge of how to live, how to get shrift, where to find Christ, how to worship Him and how to die in His arms. St. Cyril of Alexandria (*In Hosh*. iv. 6) taunts the Jews with this want of knowledge, in words that fit closelier to modern Christians, for we " have rejected the knowledge of Christ, through Whom alone the Father is accessible and knowable," we have " fatally forgotten the laws of God," nor do we " know even Moses spiritually," and our " track is not in Christ's discipline."

For all this vainly elaborate " religious education " is not in the least scriptural, for all the Jewish chronicle in it. The scriptural method is, first to show children the Passover, and, when they ask, explain it (Exod. xii. 26). Tell them the moral rules of thumb, when they ask why

The Church and the Children

—then explain these as the conditions of freedom (Deut. vi. 24). First show them piles of stones, and then explain the same (Joshua iv. 6). And so all throughout. Nor is the opposite method reasonable. What can be the spiritual gain of a detailed knowledge of the Patriarchs to one who has no knowledge of the Faith which their rude piety began and their example nourished? If one does not know God's Humanity, what does the geography of Canaan count for, and the topography of those holy fields? What do the Judges profit if one neither knows, nor cares to know, the cardinal virtues which they illustrate? How are we bettered by reciting St. Paul's mission stations if we do not know or love the Church which sent him, or the Holy Ghost Who inspired him? Of what use to us are the Apostles torn away from the great edifice, part of whose ground-structure they are? What passes for " religious education " is a barren scholasticism, more vain and profitless than the speculations of Paschasius Radbertus *de partu Beatœ Virginis*, or the questions of Julian of Toledo as to whether fat men would look fat at Doomsday. Apparently the upholders of the pseudo-scriptural scholasticism have got a newly-revised version of their own, wherein is written, " Suffer the little children to come unto Matins." " Without sermons ye can do nothing."

If men are saved by a knowledge of Huppim and Muppim, then the martyrs burnt in Nero's tar-barrels are undoubtedly lost. Even the dignified clergy could hardly maintain that these worthies consoled themselves, in their sheets of fire, by reciting over the names of the sons of Benjamin. If the wanderings of St. Paul make up such knowledge as Christ loves, then the beloved

45

disciple can be no longer beloved, for it is unlikely that
St. John, or any of the Apostles, could pass the smallest
examination on such matters. While the children are
loaded with cram, which the saints in Paradise never
knew, they are profoundly ignorant of all that brought
those saints towards Heaven ; which was certainly not
stuffed nescience about Perga and Jehoiachin.

Even as intellectual gymnastics, it is doubtful whether
this " religious education " is of the least value. " Hastie
pressing forward," says old Mulcaster, " is the greatest
enemie which anything can have whose best is to ripe
at leasure," and the man's best is to " ripe at the leasure "
of God's eternity. The hurried, unhappy, and servile
" religious education " is but lost time. Huppim and
Muppim fade away and leave not a wrack behind.
" Whatsoever the mind doth learn unwillingly with fear,
the same it doth quickly forget without care " (Ascham),
and this is especially true of St. Paul's second missionary
journey. But what the child does not forget is his dis-
taste for the dry Rabbinical lore, which is heaped in dusty
disorder over the fresh fountain-springs of Christian grace.

Consider what, in this England, used to be meant by
religious education. St. Cuthbert did not hesitate to
explain it to his Priests. In the 10th Canon of A.D. 747,
he bids them " construe and explain to the people in our
own tongue, the Creed and the Lord's Prayer and the
Sacred Words which are solemnly pronounced at the cele-
bration of the Mass and in the office of Baptism." Elfric's
Canons of A.D. 957 add the Gospel on Sundays and Mass
days. Three years later St. Dunstan (17 and 22) bids
every man " accustom his child to Christianity " (which
meant take him to Mass), " and teach him the *Pater-*

46

The Church and the Children

noster and the *Credo*, yea, and to know these things himself, as he desires to lie in holy ground, or to be worthy of the Housel." If anyone wants to know how clear, how simple, how elemental and how sacramental was the religious education thus enjoined, let him glance at the Early English Text Society's *Twelfth Century English Homilies*, and read the explanation of the *Pater* and *Credo*. This was the teaching which lasted for centuries, and did for baron and serf alike. Or take the A B C book of 1538 (reprinted by Elliot Stock), and look at what is "right necessary for children to know." Strangely enough that is no list of Jewish kings or apostolic halting-places, but directly after the alphabet these few keys to worship, *In Nomine Patris*, *Pater Noster*, *Ave Maria*, *Credo*, *Confiteor*, *Misereatur*, *Ajutorium*, *Kyrie*, *Sursum Corda*, with a few graces and thanks for ferias, fish days and Easter. Not a suspicion of Huppim, nor a breath of Baasha, nor a word of Perga and Pamphilia.

The Reformers, though it is the fashion in High Church circles to abuse them, did not, like their critics, largely depart from old English practice. In the fresh enthusiasm of a newly-opened Bible we should expect to find Huppim somewhat to the fore, and the Jewish kings brought into battle against English religion. The poor Reformers have much to answer for, but they never made themselves quite so ridiculous as their revilers pretend. Indeed they were far more enlightened than are our diocesan committees for promoting the blessed knowledge of St. Paul's stoppages. Jewel, for instance, in his treatise, *Of the Sacraments* (ii. 1127, Parker Society, as are the other references), sketches religious education as he under-

47

stood it, beginning with some nursery knowledge of God,
going on to Holy Baptism and the mystery of the Lord's
Supper, and thence into scriptural studies. Even Bul-
linger (ii. p. 293) puts a knowledge of the meaning of the
Sacraments where Barak and Eli now reign supreme :
while Cranmer (ii. 414), in his letter addressed to
Edward VI in A.D. 1548, emphatically declares that in
the Commandments of God, the Creed, and the Lord's
Prayer " is shortly and plainly included the necessary
knowledge of the whole sum of Christ's religion, and of
all things appertaining unto everlasting life." This list
might be extended almost indefinitely (Grindal, 124 ;
Ridley, 320 ; Becon, ii. 9, &c.), but for the fact that most
of our religious educationalists repudiate these writers as
authorities, and those who profess to admire them always
stop short of imitation.

If we come to inquire what instruction the modern
English Church insists upon, and how she thinks this
instruction should be given, we have not only the Church
Catechism to tell us the former, but also the 59th Canon
(1603), and the Rubrics to guide us, as to the latter. By
the Canon the Parish Priest is straitly commanded to
catechise every Sunday and holy day. If he neglects this
(and those who are filling the air with shrieks and wails
about religious education always do neglect it) he is to be
sharply reproved by the Bishop, for a second offence suspended, and for a third excommunicated. The teaching
is not of Huppim, but a plain tale of what to give up,
what to believe, and how to worship God ; things too
simple, apparently, for modern minds. What worlds of
hypocrisy and fussiness we should be saved, if this simple
act of canonical obedience were enforced upon our clerical

The Church and the Children

anarchists! "But," say our reverend canon-smashing divines, "this canon was drawn up before the elementary education system was born, and refers to a wholly different state of society." Exactly; but if an absolutely illiterate people could learn enough in one weekly half-hour's catechising, much more easily can a better-educated people acquire, by the same means, all that is necessary for the perfect life. This is both too easy a thought and too difficult an exertion for our aspiring clergymen. Where would then be the need of political agitation? the collection of great sums of money? and the blowing of trumpets and the banging of tom-toms? It can be effected without taxing schismatics, without wrecking the national chicken-fatting establishments, without a diocesan syllabus, and the rushing of rural deans; in a word, without all the lashing and splashing and hustling which is required in order to bring our youth into the clear light of Baasha and a knowledge of the missionary journeys.

To anyone who is not awake to the importance of the subject, a diocesan syllabus is a most humorous document. The Bath and Wells programme is a typical instance in point. It sketches out a nine years' course, and is so dexterously arranged that under it a child may reach the age of ten without getting as much sacramental teaching as a mediæval weanling got in a week. Yet it is not one jot worse than the syllabus of any of the five Western Dioceses, and a great deal better than some, *e.g.* than the present use of Sarum. We begin with the Creation and imbibe the Flood; we track the patriarchs over the desert, measure the Israelites' camp, and with unflagging vigour march forward to the very rebuilding of the second Temple. In a similar fashion we tackle the New Testament, dividing

God's Co-operative Society

the Scriptures into ninety huge slabs, which are meted out as the children's bread. There is no mercy in the matter. We begin with the earth without form and void, and end, of course, with the second missionary journey. In addition to all this, we study Matins (a devotion written for monks and nuns, and therefore peculiarly suited for the youthful laity), and the seasons of the Christian year. Next year we broach Evensong in our ascetic zeal, and obtain a general knowledge of the Litany. In the third year those who have attained the age of eight and a half are promoted to a still deeper study of the Litany. Children of ten, however, are allowed to study the Ante-Communion Service, by which is meant the Ante-non-Communion, after which they begin again to re-mumble the bones of Matins. But surely they learn the Church Catechism? some one will say. Yes; and that is certainly something, except that up to the age of ten years old they only get as far as " the desire," and never learn what is " generally necessary to salvation." Later on they take the whole Catechism " with Scripture proofs," and the monitors actually advance to a study of types; and at last, at the eleventh hour, and after years of fruitless research, they are invited to study what the mediæval children and little reformers began with—the whole Communion Service. This invitation is very rarely accepted, for they leave upon the earliest possible opportunity, and the monitors are lured far afield into the ample pastures of Church History, and may there pick up any sort of lore, except the not unimportant knowledge of how to meet their God.[1]

[1] Since this criticism was published the diocese has mended its ways. Once in three years, children of the Third and Fourth Standard

The Church and the Children

Now, every child christened in an English church is bound to go to the Sacrament, because it is ordered to hear sermons, and the only rubrical place for a sermon is at the Sacrament, and this would surely be the simplest and pleasantest form of religious education, if our Puritan grimness will allow of such adjectives. But the modern topsy-turvey syllabus lays stress upon everything in inverse proportion to its value, and consequently our course ends with private devotions and hymns, for hymns always flourish largely when heresies are rife.

Therefore, while our clergy are coaxing and caballing, petitioning Parliament, charging and plaguing everybody about private schools and voluntary schools as the one and only means of life and light for the English ; while they are instant in season and out of season, with rates or without them, to proclaim the glories of Huppim and Muppim and Ard, the people are destroyed for lack of knowledge. Congregations turn their backs upon Christ's precious Blood, reject His Body, scoff at the remission of sins and the Sacrament of Penance. They do not hew out for themselves anything so dignified as a broken cistern, but they scratch out, each man for himself, paltry little puddles, which they call their religion and their " views." They are the prey of quack-salvers and charlatans, false prophets from whom Huppim and Muppim are impotent to defend them. They know all about Abraham except the way to his bosom ; all about David except his sure mercies ; and all about St.

are now invited to study the Communion Office, and the Sacramental part of the Catechism is given to all in the Fifth Standard. It would be delightful to think ╎that six per cent. of the scholars know the Ter Sanctus.

God's Co-operative Society

Paul except the Faith which he preached and which justified him.

What hold has Anglicanism got upon the ordinary Anglican ? None whatever. A Roman Catholic will spend ten solitary years in the Australian bush and be faithful to his religion, and return to it on the first opportunity ; but his English brother cannot be trusted for ten minutes near a strange conventicle or he will quickly go a-whoring after the dreary gods of division and negation, despite his probable knowledge of the missionary journeys.

Contrary to the opinion of those great Cambridge divines, whose one message to mankind is to read the Greek Testament in uncials, and avoid profane swearing, it must be asserted that the knowledge which saves is small and easily gotten. It is not God's will that all His people should climb the steep heights of logical difficulty or ford the deep streams of learning and research. Gentlemen who know Hebrew and Greek and Latin—like Pontius Pilate, Bunyan says—are too apt to forget that it is not by grammar, or geography, not by sound reasoning and correct glossing upon the name of Huppim, not by rote knowledge of antique travels, that the Lord wills His people to enter into life. The narrow way and the strait gate may be small, but they are simple. The one is not a maze and the other is not fitted with ingenious and complicated locks. By all means let whosoever has leisure and inclination rack the Scriptures and revel in the geography of Asia Minor, let anyone number and date the kings, disentangle the very secrets of the Apocalypse, and distinguish Lebbæus from Thaddæus, but none of these things is religious education. If there is anything in the teaching of the historical Christian religion, there must be glorious

52

companies, goodly fellowships, noble armies, and holy saints walking in glory, who knew nothing of all this "religious education," but who merely knew how to live and how to worship, how to wash their robes white in the Lamb's Blood, and how to die fortified with all the antidotes against death and hell.

The conclusion therefore may be easily drawn. It does not matter a bit, as far as religious education goes, whether we have secular provided schools, or whether we have non-provided schools or no schools at all. It matters very much indeed that we should recognise that real religious education is not being given now and never will be given, so long as we attempt boundlessly too much and vitally too little.

AND ARD

It has generally been admitted, not only by great numbers of the inferior clergy, but by many grave and religious writers, even by many of the dignified divines of the Church, that Huppim and Muppim have hitherto played a disproportionate part in the religious education of the English children. But this admission by no means implies reform, or even penitence. Indeed, he would be a very sanguine physician who hoped to cure a disease by enumerating its symptoms and evil effects, however summary and efficient this enumeration might be. The symptoms of the disease are the sad substitution of Huppim and Muppim for Christian Faith and Worship, the deplorable *sequelæ* are spiritual lassitude and nausea, followed by a depraved appetite for schism and negation or by an utter loss of appetite even for the delicacies of the Divine banquet.

God's Co-operative Society

It is not enough to point to these and other like facts: for before any treatment can be suggested, it is necessary to go back behind *sequelæ* and symptoms to the efficient causes of the distress. These are evidently to be looked for as concentrated in the clergy themselves. And here it is a matter which requires some niceness of handling, for who would wish to be found beating his fellow-servants?

Assuredly there is something wrong in the clergy, and evidently that something is not a question of character or of general intelligence. In spite of all the overmuch blaming to which they are subjected, there is no body of men who so pathetically and rapturously long to do right. There is no body of men known to the public who are so generally and so rightly trusted and sought out in any matter which sheer honesty and ready kindness can effect. As to general intelligence they are still *stupor mundi*, as in the disastrous seventeenth century. Whatever learned Society a man consults, he is sure to meet there a good proportion of clerical names. Wherever his studies lead him he will find the way already marked by boots obviously clerical. Yet the clergy are fighting a losing battle, and are doggedly and heroically holding ground which exposes them defenceless to every blackguard who chooses to fire a cheap pistol into their sable ranks, ground which makes them less than a match for their most contemptible and lightest opponents. With the spirit of a martyr, the learning of a cultured Englishman, and the zeal of a dervish, the clergyman (Huppim in hand) rushes upon the children of his parishioners, intent to gather them in; and behold he merely straws them to all the winds.

It seems obvious that Huppim and Muppim must have been bred in the bone of the clergy, before these could come out so conspicuously in the flesh ; and therefore the coign of discomfiture is to be looked for in the training given to the clergy themselves. Let any man compare the theory of the English Ordinal, with the actual recruiting and training of the English clergy, in each grade, and he will be surprised to see that these have little or nothing in common.

The Prayer Book implies that the Deacon is chosen because by nature, learning, and morals he is apt for his work. That work is to give help in the great drama of Public and Common Worship, especially in that of the Holy Communion. He is to read aloud, to teach the catechism, possibly to baptize, maybe to preach, and assuredly to favour the work of the Church among the poor. By nature, he is assumed to be the kind of man who will need the curbs suggested in the Epistle of his Ordination. These point to persons of a jovial caste of mind, shrewd, not unversed in the wiles of women, business-like, and able to cope with the *banderlog* of boys. His acquirements then must be a mastery of the form and content of Public Worship, an articulate and resonant intonation, some such sense of discipline as a pupil teacher is required to show, an expert knowledge of Baptism, a capacity to talk sense if he be loosed upon a congregation, and an acquaintance with social problems, with much leaning to the poor man's side of the question. Actually he is examined in none of these matters. The first qualification for the office of a deacon is to have been educated in a public school and to have graduated at a University, where none of these things are learnt. The deacon must have a social distinctness and know the importance of apt tailoring and genteel speech. He must be the master of

certain facts, such as the use of *quin*, that *nolo* and not
recuso is Latin for " I refuse." He must be on calling terms
with the world. It does him no harm to have a few
fallacies about him. He may believe, for instance, that the
masses do like a gentleman to lead them, which is a state-
ment falsified alike by modern facts and by a mere refer-
ence to the ancient fishermen, tentmakers and tramps, who
subdued kingdoms and whose successors might be supposed
to be above such nonsense.[1]

Now there is no body of boys so flagrantly ignorant of
Christian learning, as the students of our public schools.
The religious training, relegated by perplexed parents to
still more puzzled pedagogues, might excite the Basutos
to derision. A slight acquaintance with Mac Somebody's
Old Testament History, with a few comments weakly
remembered from Stanley's *Jewish Church*, complete one
part of the course. The second part is concluded by a
few scrappy lessons upon the Greek of the Gospels, with
animadversion upon St. John's lean use of particles, and
a generally implied notion that a little more correction
from Codex Aleph and a little less insistence upon Faith
would cheer us all up immensely. These are the religious
acquirements of the Sixth Form boy, who proceeds, thus
lightly equipped, to the University. Here he learns that
there are nine-and-thirty Articles, patient of any sense or
of none. He attends certain professorial lectures (in the
pauses of which he may hear the words " I go nap ") and he
gleans a little information that Baron Von Soden and other
German gentlemen are making sport with theologians and

---

[1] Is it our profound humility which makes us believe that if we
waive our claim to be accounted gentlemen and squires minor, we
shall have no other possible claim to be revered ?

The Church and the Children

Church historians and with devout believers generally.
But he minds them not. He inclines to do good and yearns
for the status and opportunity of the English parson.
He consults a prelate, who snaps him up and whether
directly, or through the medium of a theological college,
suggests a short course of study, which is determined,
and may be gauged, by the bishops' examination papers.
Bearing in mind St. Paul's requirements of a deacon,
let any unbiassed man peep into these papers. Here
are some ten questions actually set of late in our most
enlightened and important diocese :

1. Explain the symbols P, JE, SS, and D.
2. Distinguish Commemoration and Memorial.
3. Say what you know of the principles underlying the
English Calendar.[1]
4. What does Row consider to be the most useful argument in discussing Christian Evidences ?
5. Comment upon " Lo ! we heard of it at Ephrathah."
6. What can you say (*in seven minutes and a half*) of
the philosophical and theological use of the word substance ?
7. What conception of the Person of Christ should we
draw from the synoptic Gospels alone ?
8. Describe the geographical position of Decapolis.
9. Parse six Hebrew verbs.
10. What does England owe to the Irish Missions ?

It is obvious that these are not questions for deacons
at all, but for priests and theologians in the making. But
lest they should be supposed to be the fads of one fallible
prelate, let them be compared with the preliminary ques-

[1] Surely an enemy hath set this !

57

tions for deacons, that is to say with the questions set by
the co-operative society of examining bishops :

1. Where was Nob ?
2. Examine the foreign policy of Ahab.
3. Comment upon " Moab is my washpot."
4. What date would *you* assign to the Epistle of St.
James ?
5. Explain clearly the heresy of Nestorius.
6. Explain the term " shawm."
7. Sum up the gains and losses from the establishment
of Christianity, as a State Religion. (*This is a sprynge
to catch woodcocks.*)
8. Who were the Non-jurors ?
9. Translate a few snacks of St. Augustine, of the Kings
in Hebrew, and of the same book from the LXX.

These are specimens from the whole papers. Not a
word about reading, voice-production, music, not a sug-
gestion of slums, sweating, soup kitchens, balance sheets,
truck acts, sanitation, allotments, diseases, and school
teaching. Not a hint at the first principles of stage
management, without which all public functions, civil or
religious, are apt to be ridiculous. Not a question as to
how to christen a child validly, an art which might be
thought to be of some use to deacons.

But let us grant that we have done wisely and well
when we abolished the diaconate by making it nothing
but a porch to the priesthood. The priests' work according to the Ordinal is to teach, feed, and search out, to
forgive sins and to bless. It is difficult to see how this
mastery of Shawms, Nob, Katal, and Company, are more
than agreeable accomplishments, which like billiards and

The Church and the Children

the Mazurka may be useful, as all accomplishments are useful, provided that they are kept in strict subordination and used as the sauces of life rather than its roast meats. But does the priest know his proper work? Obviously he knows every craft under the sun except priestcraft.

The playing-fields of Eton have a real place in history: most of our battles have been lost there. Our other academies, however, do not lag far behind. They too are thick sown with disaster. Here the young soldier learnt that so long as he plays a good forward in football, it is unnecessary to have any scientific knowledge of men, weapons, tactics, or strategy. Here too the future priest learnt that the Church is best served by him who can bowl a maiden Over. Really, why need one know what to teach, so long as Huppim is in such great request and Muppim is accepted as the only miraculous food for infants? If one is but a gentleman one has no need to seek out. One is naturally attractive, especially to the masses—just as Dr. Wolff was naturally clean. As for sins, the priest often does not know even which of them are deadly and which venial. Sometimes he disbelieves that he can or ought to forgive them. In blessings, he does not know one from another, nor all from their opposites. He gaily gives the Eucharistic blessing, and the Pax too, after Evensong and at the Mothers' Meeting. He does not know how to absolve, nor how to move men to confession. He cannot prepare anyone for Baptism, Confirmation, Communion, Unction, or Death. How often, it may be asked, does the average clergyman dine out, and what ghostly counsel does he give to his fellow-diners, that the whole of his education should be directed towards making him

God's Co-operative Society

into a genteel table-companion for the squire and the resident gentry ? Is it quite worth while to sacrifice the saving knowledge of the Gospel, all the spiritual education of the people, and the whole work of the priesthood, in order that our Aarons may be able to keep the mansion table in a roar, without the least indecency ? Granted the supreme importance of this social art, yet would it not be better to have it distributed impartially ? Should not some be called to this holy function, who could set the commercial room, the bar, and even the tap-room in a roar, even if such ate fish with a knife and sniffed during Bridge ? Since each priest could not be, like Cæsar's wife, all things to all men, should we not have chaplains to other men ? to retail traders, dentists, and marines ? as well as chaplains to landed gentlemen ? Possibly the three million families of poor too, might be allowed a few chaplains, while still at large, in addition to their prison chaplains ? But this will seem Utopian and a digression.

After the education for his office described above, the priest sallies forth to uphold a falling Church, prepared to do, or at least to die, in defence of the Establishment (which he often mistakes for the Church)—" his drawn salary in his hand." The figures, with the cool malignity of their kind, show how he manages the task.

Whereas the population between 1898 and 1902 increased by 2,934,137 persons, the Church was only increased by 14,989 additional baptisms (or one in 195). The Confirmations showed a falling off of 9459 and the Ordination Candidates, instead of increasing, fell by 76. Though the communicants are estimated to have increased by 182,791, this is a very doubtful estimate, many people in their

60

The Church and the Children

returns giving the number of Communions made, rather than the number of communicants. That our bishops are diminishing in proportion to the population may be gauged by one fact, viz. that if we were bishoped up to the standard of Queen Elizabeth's day and of the blessed Reformation, we should have two archbishops and thirty-six bishops for London alone. This hardly looks as though a clergy dieted upon Shawms, Nob, Washpots, and gentility were effective, or that a laity dieted upon Huppim and Muppim were responsive. What esteem would the medical profession hold with the public if the surgeons slurred over the homely arts of dressing and dispensing, compared with clapping alphabets to their names and displaying a nice knowledge of Egyptian dentistry ? Yet these homely arts are their diaconate. As St. Gregory points out, in his *Cura Pastoralis*, " Who does not know that the wounds of men's thoughts are deeper than those of their bowels ? Yet not seldom, those who know not the practice of the Spirit will not shrink from professing the leechdom of the heart, while those who know not the virtues of pigments would blush to be called healers of the flesh."

If the clergy, then, are trained, or not trained, to the tune of bishops' examinations, it is but logical to ask how the bishops themselves are chosen ? and trained ? And here again the theory of the Ordinal is flatly contradicted by the practice of the State.

The list of Pauline cautions for bishops seems to point to a set of men quite different from those moderate and discreet gentlemen whom the civil Government delights to honour, and whom the Prime Minister (lately a Dissenter who disbelieved in bishops, and soon to be one who also disbelieves in a Church and even possibly in a

God's Co-operative Society

God) appoints to the charge of Christ's visible kingdom. The Apostle, when he advised these holy fathers, thinks it necessary to warn them not to be too dashing and devil-may-care, to restrain their runaway enthusiasm for girls, to limit their hearty eupeptic sleep, to master their vigorous appetites, to keep within bounds, to love foreigners, to help lame dogs. They are to stop at the third glass, to keep their knuckles out of other folk's faces, to be genuine, unpeevish, above the passion for endowments, holding Mrs. Bishop in, with a tight rein and having the naughty little bishops well in hand. Should St. Paul not rather have warned them against excess in tea and mineral waters and gossip ? Should he not have dropped some admonitions against being safe men in any other sense than that of the Athanasian Creed ? Is it conceivable that he forgot to tell them to regard the Faith not as botanists poring over an *herbarium siccum*, but as men who had the audacity to use it ? Why did he not warn them against the light frivolities of Shawms, Nob, and Washpots ? and spice his words with objurgations against the World, as well as the Flesh ? It is obvious that he was eyeing a different stamp of man from those who now adorn and polish the Bench, to wit, heavy, hearty, muscular, bass-voiced men, who took life with voracity, who knew little of the sweets of flattery, of chaplains, and decorum ; men who were like, and often were, village blacksmiths rather than college dons. Indeed Celsus depicts them, when he describes the Christians, as the sort of men you would collect to make a band of robbers. What had these old stalwarts to teach ? The miracles peculiar to St. Luke had not been recorded. Poor Moses was not yet discovered to be a joint-stock company under an *alias*. Isaiah had met the

The Church and the Children

literal but not the literary sawyers. Dearly-beloved-brethren had not been patched together. The Nestorian controversy still slept. Even the second missionary journey was sixteen years old and not in the least venerable. There was no office of Matins, nor of Evensong. These unfortunate and boxing bishops could only have had for their curriculum, Humility and the Incarnation, Hope and the Resurrection, Faith and the Ascension, Charity and the Blessed Trinity, Worship and the Cause of the Poor. Their examination papers then must have differed considerably from ours. They could not ask candidates the nett gains of the Establishment and gravel them if they saw none. Yet there is no record that out of sheer lack of vitality they had to fall back upon Muppim, Huppim, and Ard. No doubt these heroes were in the reserve, but they were the last line of defence, and it must be admitted that they were not then needed in the fighting line of the Church militant and pugilist, which yet somehow did what we do not and went forward. Is it possible that the wrong man chooses the wrong men for the episcopate ?

There seems to be no provision for training bishops, no staff College : and it is not our use to supply an honest, shrewd man to jog one elbow, while a trained theologian jogs the other, which was the mediæval plan. It has been suggested that the Athenæum Club really supplies all these needs, although even that may be disputed.

A venerable dean and an imaginative canon, panting to see Truth without her trappings, have lately been imploring us to rule out everything that is not primitive, and we are asked to go back bodily to those six golden centuries when (they feel quite certain) the Holy Ghost still lived and worked. But have they counted the agonies of bereavement into which they would plunge us ? If we have to give up chasubles, what about frock coats and top hats ? Will these abide this arbitrary date ? If amices are torn from us, what about the garb of gentility ? When dalmatics fail, how shall diocesan syllabuses abide ? What will happen to the course of studies at the fifteen theological colleges ? What would be left for deacons to pass ? Are deaneries and canonries to survive only in their primitive forms ? If the tackle of Worship shrinks, these august offices will also collapse into cells. The Arch-presbyter of Canterbury and his Cænobite brother, unendowed, unwived, unhousemaided, gnawing feebly at a diet of raw radishes, will shrink in proportional diameter. And worst of all we should lose the main-stays of our religious education, both Huppim, Muppim, and Ard.

Still some reform seems to be needed, throughout the Church : and before trying the drastic methods of those melancholics who would give us Wizardry, Buddhism, or Totemism for the Faith of our fathers, it might be worth while to try whether our disease is not merely dyspepsia, caused by a hard and stony food given us in huge slabs in our youth. If so, our nursing clergy require to be trained for their work, and themselves fostered in nursery management. But their work is meted out to them by their fathers in God, who again are not trained for their own work and do not organise the work of others upon the lines of faith, reason, and experience. This, we are told, is one of the consequences of the priceless blessings of the Establishment which gives us the wrong men, with the wrong methods, and fills the Church militant with hunger, tremors, and indigestion. The conclusion

The Church and the Children

of the whole matter seems simple, namely, that these priceless blessings are very heavily priced, are no blessings at all, but very far from it. In a word, that the Establishment is an unclean thing, and actively poisonous.

CHAPTER IV

THE CHURCH AND SOCIAL PROBLEMS. I. PRESENT
AND FUTURE

THERE can be no doubt that Churchmen, as such, are
bound to be both political and social in their aims. When
once it is admitted that we are our brother's keeper and
that he is our brother, the Rubicon is passed. The terms
of the Baptismal Covenant, the Lord's Prayer itself, and
the visibility of Heaven's Kingdom, all coerce the mind
by irresistible logic to accept an earthly expression for
the heavenly vision, to accept a responsibility for all
that can be moulded and remoulded by human hands
and human minds nearer to the heart's desire of God, for
all that can be destroyed and still remains, of what He
disdains and disapproves. It is true that our citizenship
is in heaven, but earth is either its sacrament, or a sacrament of some quite other and opposite kingdom, which
we are bound to oppose. The consistent Protestant is of
course an individualist and an anarchist. He is surprised,
bored, and perhaps scornful of laws, lawgivers, and taxes.
If he touches these matters it is in a byplay, as he might
smoke or play tennis; as relaxation, athletic or medicinal,
for the mind; but his immortal soul is alone and apart.
If the poor are unhappy, it is either their own fault for
being drunken and work-shy, or else God moves in a
mysterious way and it is a slight matter. The sorrow lasts

66

only for an infinitesimal fraction of eternity. Let them sweat!

But with the Catholic it is not so. He sees everything stamped with the mark of eternal significance. He belongs to a State that he is proud to remember has warred with great empires and worsted them. He cannot say, " Let the king, lords, and commons do what they like." That would be to admit that the saints were fools and knaves, when they defied the imperial law of combinations, refused the civil ceremonies, revised the decrees of senates, and imposed the enactments of love and common sense upon a proud and indocile people. The most startling result of the Revolution of 1688 was the withdrawal of our clergy from the political and social spheres. That is to say, they withdrew as religious men, and having no faith to guide them, accepted the commands and coaxes of the rulers of things as they are. They became the toadies and servitors of the rich and insolent, of the great families, who impaired both Crown and Commons for their own advancement.

Then came that great wrong, the overthrow and downfall of the agricultural labourer, which began with science and ended in grab and brutality, in starvation, despair, ineffective revolt, and bitter memories which are still a grievous hindrance to a wise polity. If a man names this evil period and asks of the Christian leaders: What were you doing all this time? our faces will be more ashamed than when all the nonsense about Galileo and the civil martyrs is heaped together to confound us.

The story is in brief this, but it may be read at length in J. and B. Hammond's book, *The Village Labourer* (Longmans). The agriculture of England was communal, in arable, pasture, and waste, roughly speaking, until the accession of George III. This applies to about six-sevenths of the whole. By 3700 acts these common lands were enclosed. The small holders were ruined and dispossessed. The labourers were forced to depend wholly on their day labour. Their real wages fell to starvation point. They had no fuel, no milk, no games, and no recreation. They took to poaching and the Game Laws resulted ; they took to theft and robbery and the Criminal Laws made it capital to steal five shillings worth of goods. They were given out-relief, and were thus chained to the land by pauper settlements. They burnt machines and rebelled and were hanged, sent to the hulks, to Botany Bay, &c. Both Whigs and Tories were equally zealous to steal the common from the goose. With bread at a shilling a loaf and wages down to seven shillings per week, with children eating swedes and horse beans, it is a wonder the race survived. But the clergy, with few exceptions, allowed or even helped this cruel and bloody conspiracy. Even men like Sydney Smith protested against man-traps and spring-guns, but asked indignantly if farmers are not to get labour as cheap as they can, and saw no reason why they should not do so, if they could.[1] In 1727 Chamberlayne remarks how sturdy the English common people are, that " after twelve hours' hard work, they will go to football, stoolball, cricket, prison-base, wrestling, cudgel-playing, or some such vehement exercise." In 1827 the children were gaunt and cowed creatures, fed on barley meal, and a herring was sometimes divided between eight of them.

The two great religious movements which came on the heels of this wicked revolution were the Evangelical and

---

[1] " Poor Laws." *E. Review,* 1820.

The Church and Social Problems

the Tractarian. The former, to its credit and glory, associated itself with social reforms and the latter with something far more deep and stable, the associative principle.

The Evangelicals supported the entire change of the prisons, and from that, the wiser and humaner treatment of young offenders. They were zealous to abolish chattel slavery and to educate the people in Sunday-schools, when the day-school system was hardly born. They were great against profusion and self-indulgence. In Thomas Scott we can see one of the best and most typical at work. He gave medicine to the poor and was a keen reformer in hospital and infirmary matters. He and others after him prepared the way for later improvements, like the Factory Acts. He was unworldly, and both advocated and practised giving away as much as he laid by, which alms he called "seed corn." But neither his largeness of heart, nor the ale, which he kept to refresh the bodies and open the ears of his visitors, did anything to arrest the tragic fall of the labourer, with which his whole pastoral life coincided (1772–1821). The same is true of the later movement. It accomplished some good and great things which endeared it to the English public; but they were sporadic and isolated. The Islington party, which was born of Clapham, inherited the exclusiveness, the hatred of amusements, and the impoverishment of life which marred the teaching of the earlier adherents; but they retained none of that social reforming spirit, which won the respect of all good persons.

The Tractarians, on the other hand, saw and taught the associative principle, which is and has always been a governing one in the Church of history. They began at the altar.

God's Co-operative Society

They tried to set the household of faith in order. They drew attention to the misunderstood doctrines, the broken discipline, the neglected decencies, and the belittled claims of the Church. They fought manfully and crusadingly for great ideas, which were to make beautiful the Church, but they did not inquire if these would also make beautiful the street, the shop, market, law-court, and gymnasium. It was not their task. They too had successors, who mimicked their tones and wore their clothes, but never extended, except ecclesiologically, the application of those great and (as they were felt to be) subversive principles, of which the world was genuinely apprehensive.

The fate of the Evangelicals has befallen the Puseyites. The disciples have lost the conquering and extending spirit. They are content with their fathers' winnings.

If there were a Broad Church Party the same would be true of that. "The form of Christianity which because it is not intellectual is called muscular" has broken into dust. Not only the gospel of muscles and marriage has vanished; but such Parson Lots as we may have, are not Christian Socialists in Kingsley's sense of the term at all, and are certainly not liberal thinkers. The highly superior modernists are not found in trades union halls and on street tubs, but are ancient enough to be owners of shares in companies, which are neither co-operative nor eleemosynary, nor even merciful. Their coats were certainly not made by the co-operative tailors, nor are their teachings in the least exasperating to Semites and company-promoters. Mr. Kingsley has taken Father Newman's advice and flown away.

The application of Catholic principles to political and social questions was not the task of the Tractarians, but

The Church and Social Problems

they admitted it frankly enough. They had no notion that Church principles, which began at the altar, stopped at the south porch or the lych-gate. If any man will read Pusey's sermons on " Why did Dives lose his soul ? " and " The Danger of Riches," [1] and compare them with those of other preachers, he will be astonished at the boldness of social application. Let him not take SS. Augustine or Gregory Magnus, but men like Luther, Bunyan, Keach, Milner, Simeon, and Trench, or to vary the research, Tillotson, Wake, Sherlock, and Laurence Sterne, all of whom have published their thoughts on the parable. It will be at once evident that a seemingly new and certainly bold spirit has informed the Tractarian leader. He applies his faith to social and economic questions as this had not been done in England, at least since the times of the Stuarts.

Take Newman, who to us seems the great genius of the whole movement. Though in a private letter to the present writer he declared he had never considered social questions in their relation to faith, and had always looked upon the poor as objects for compassion and benevolence, yet in his history of the Arians [2] he makes short work of the non-political believer and all his tremblings.

" Strictly speaking, the Christian Church, as being a visible society, is necessarily a political power and party. It may be a party triumphant or a party under persecution ; but a party it must always be, prior in existence to the civil institutions with which it is surrounded, and from its latent divinity formidable and influential even to the end of time. The grant of permanency was made in the

---

[1] *Lenten Sermons, II.; Occasional Sermons,* 1850.
[2] Pt. II. cap. iii. p. 264.

beginning, not to the mere doctrine of the Gospel, but to the Association itself, built upon the doctrine (St. Matt. xvi. 18); in prediction not only of the indestructibility of Christianity, but of the medium also through which it was to be manifested to the world. Thus the ecclesiastical body is a divinely-appointed means towards realising the great Evangelical blessings. Christians depart from their duty, or become in an offensive sense political, not when they act as members of one community, but when they do so for temporal ends or in an illegal manner; not when they assume the attitude of a party, but when they split into many. If the primitive believers did not interfere with the acts of the civil Government, it was merely because they had no rights enabling them legally to do so. But where they have rights the case is different (Acts xvi. 37–39); and the existence of a secular spirit is to be ascertained not by their using these, but their using them for ends short of the ends for which they were given. Doubtless in criticising the mode of their exercising them in a particular case, differences of opinion may fairly exist; but the principle itself, the duty of using their civil rights in the service of religion, is clear; and since there is a popular misconception that Christians, and especially the clergy as such, have no concern in temporal affairs, it is expedient to take every opportunity of formally denying the position, and demanding a proof of it. In truth the Church was framed for the express purpose of interfering, or (as irreligious men will say) meddling with the world. It is the plain duty of its members not only to associate internally, but also to develop that internal unity in an external warfare with the spirit of evil, whether in king's courts, or among the mixed multitude; and if they can do nothing else, at least they can suffer for the truth, and remind men of it, by inflicting upon them the task of persecution."

This extract is peculiarly strong, for Newman himself was, in the political sense, a complete aristocrat at heart, and far too nice in taste to find any pleasure in the dust of the political arena. He cannot be accused of enjoying political scuffle first and justifying it afterwards.

It is worth while to notice that, in this passage from Newman, we have an instance of the Platonism of the Tractarians. It was not the least of the services, which that splendid company of men did for the Church of England, that they brought back the thoughts, alas! not of the laity but of a large section of the clergy, to Plato, and away, one must not say, from Aristotle, but from that Aristotelianism, which is rather different. That is to say, they used the Christian catch-words in the sense in which they were written: they hung the Gospel picture in the light in which it was painted. This will be clear, if we lay alongside of Newman's challenge the parallel from the end of the ninth book of the Republic of Plato, where the genuine votary of the just and ordered state is described as having his eyes constantly fixed upon that. Glaucon remarks:

"Then assuredly, if this is his chief care, he will not be willing to touch politics.

By the dog, said I, but he will, in his own country, and that vigorously, but maybe not in the land of his birth, unless some divine prompting be laid upon him.

I understand, said he. You are speaking of the country we have now settled in our description, which is founded in reasoning, for I fancy it exists nowhere else in the world.

God's Co-operative Society

Yes, I said, but maybe the pattern of it is treasured in heaven for him who wishes to behold it, and beholding, to plant himself therein as its colonist. What does it matter whether it exists or will exist ? He will touch the politics of this country alone and of none other at all.

Yes, it seems so, he replied."

This City of God, this juster social and political order, which Plato and his successors saw eternal in the heavens, the Christian Church saw not in that great, though accessible height, but descending from the throne of God. If he repudiated a non-political faith, *a fortiori*, we must do so, for when the Word was made flesh, His work lies in the region where flesh suffers and is constrained, where it is governed and lifted up, or loosed and degraded.

The absolute inefficiency of the individual to help himself by himself, the consequent need of a society, a club, a country, a Church—whatever we call it—that was the root principle for which the Tractarians contested. In things spiritual this leads to all their principal doctrines. Man is broken into men : that is the fall. Men must be united into man ; that is the need of Baptism and its regeneration. They are united by God's grace ; that is the Church, the Apostolic Succession, and the unity of the Faith. They are constantly liable to fall from this unity and can be restored ; that is absolution and penance. They are united in a living whole, which needs constant feeding and building up ; that is the whole Sacramental system. This work can only be done by the perfect and archetypal man ; that is the Real Presence and the miracle of the Mass, to be set forth with all that is solemn and impressive, with all the appeals to each gate of the soul, the organs of sense, eye-gate, ear-gate, nose-gate, and so

74

The Church and Social Problems

on ; that is the meaning and use of ritual. All these teachings are of a piece and go together. But the man who tries to think in a straight line cannot stop here. The anarchy he combats in things of religion, he will suspect and oppose in the outward world. The bread, which is transformed until it becomes the highest gift of God, the drink which becomes the essence of the atonement, will cause him to ask, what invisible thing also lies behind the cottage loaf and the dinner beer. It has been well said the generation which despises the bread of God cannot get an unadulterated loaf at the baker's and the people who mock at the wine of heaven cannot get a glass of ale made without substitutes. Then this bread and this beer, it is evident, are outward and visible signs of some inward and spiritual disgrace.

A man, who has been sojourning in his own country, the New Jerusalem, and learned his fraternity, its unity with itself, cannot lightly or logically see the predatory society outside and conform to it immediately and without qualms. If he has been a colonist in the land, which is free and the mother of us all, he will be ill content with a servile State, or a gross and partial polity of privilege. The very test of his sincerity, and of the truth of the vision he tells us he has enjoyed, will be his outlook upon social and political problems ; whether he is patient or impatient of sullied waters of life, of healing trees cut down, of stained robes, soiled crowns, and harps jangled, of freedom sold and Christ's face-marks clean obliterated. The most serious charge which can be brought against our modern High Churchmen, is that the things they tolerate and support outside the Church clearly prove that they have not seen what they think they see inside.

God's Co-operative Society

That is why they are not only negligible in politics, ineffective in the City, impotent in all great movements, unheard upon all great questions of the day, and only half accepted, as a kind of game, by the people who profess to support them. That is why the air is full of quackery, of Nonconformist substitutes, of Christian Science, Theosophy, Buddhism, and Labour Churches, of religions of golf and motoring, of Higher Criticism and lower trumpeting, of new theories to support old sins, of pessimism stolen from Hindus, and the occult lore cabbaged from negroes.

Meantime on other planes, things are calling for men of higher zeal and seriousness. The deplorable state of politics is confessed. The gulf between Haves and Havenots is widening ceaselessly. The growing power of machinery and combination make it more impossible for the workman ever to own his tools, or to become, by thrift, his own capitalist. Class bitterness grows in bulk ; and unrest, though the anodyne of prosperity soothes it for a little, is wider, more active, and at times even maniacal. More alarming still is the sex-cleavage. The wife has lost her loom and her spinning-wheel, her still-room, mash-tub, oven, and broidery frame. The industrial evolution has taken from her not only her work, but the usefulness and the dignity and much of the honour of her life. Nor is she called upon to marry so early, bear so many children, or educate those she bears. Meanwhile with less to do, and consequently less which causes her to be honoured, she is more educated and less restrained. The result is a revolt, which surprises and disgusts the men who have unwittingly caused it ; a revolt which breaks out in unexpected places and ruins countless lives and wrecks numberless homes. The individualism of man is eagerly caught up by woman, who is indeed the individualist force in nature, and ruthlessly carried to its extremes of self-assertion and selfishness.

On every side we see all old theories cast into the melting-pot, all old customs challenged, all old legislative principles discarded, and the world in suspense waiting for the clear guidance of the only authority which can pronounce dogmatic verdicts, the Church of Christ. That Church is at present manacled and gagged. The greatest question of the time is whether she will ever obtain the use of her hand and tongue to speak the clear, saving word, for lack of which the whole earth is in jeopardy.

To forecast that word is to turn to the past; but not in any slavish spirit. The past is past, because it was out-grown. Every cry with "back" in it is self-condemned. Back to the Primitive Church, to the Middle Ages, to the Reformation, back to the land, to the Commune, to Owen or Wesley, to republican Rome or the disunited States of Greece, to the Egyptians or the Incas, to the Guilds or to Karl Marx, to the painters before Raphael or the Goths before Varrus, to the Saxons before William, or the critics before Strauss, or the music before Wagner; these are all examples of vain cries. "Back flies the foam, the hoisted flag streams back." If we look to the past, it is to see not the actualities which have disappeared, but those inset ideas, which are everlasting. We look to last year's fruit, not because we complain that it is moulded away, but to see what we may expect of the tree which bore it. We look to the tree, not because it bore fruit last year, not hoping that it is hung with fruit now, in the winter, but because if it ever bears again it will bear fruit of the same brand, though possibly better, larger, and more abundant. If the

God's Co-operative Society

Church now and in the future is to speak socially and politically, she must obviously speak as one true to herself. Therefore we must turn, with apologies, but without shame, to ask in what direction the primitive believers Newman speaks of, would have used the rights which were denied to them. The answer requires a chapter to itself.

CHAPTER V

THE teaching of these primitive believers leads us to see that they would have exercised their powers in the direction of the frankest Socialism. It is evident, indeed it is almost an axiom, that every writer who is sound and saintly declares himself wholly and unhesitatingly in favour of the common holding of goods, of equality of opportunity, and of interdependence. Even writers who are less orthodox, and consequently more inclined to favour some kinds of individualist law, are entirely at one with their more orthodox contemporaries in a fierce opposition to that covetousness, which now calls itself enterprise, smartness, exertion, thrift, push, and the like. The New Testament may be passed over, because it is in everybody's hands, and is read with such inconceivable prejudice, that most people are entirely unable to see what is there set forth. For instance, the very word "righteousness" has been pared and lopped down to mean no more than the personal virtues, whereas δικαιοσύνη has no such limitation, and would be better, for the moment, rendered " justice," in each of its eighty-six occurrences ; as its opposite, ἀδικία, used twenty-five times, would be better understood as "injustice." The stories are impaired by every perversity of gloss the wit of man can contrive. The ninth century was supposed to be a dark age, but how clear is its teaching,

God's Co-operative Society

compared with the nebulousness of the nineteenth. Take
one example, the story of the man who wished his brother
to divide the inheritance with him. To Joseph Milner it
suggested that happiness consisteth not in abundance, to
the Victorian divines that our Lord refused to pronounce
upon questions of property, but to Walafridus Strabus, the
monk of Fulda, in his *Glossa Ordinaria*, it appears thus :

" *Who made Me*, &c. I am no God of division, but of
peace and unity, who came to federate men with the
angels, that many might have one heart and one mind.
Not that things be divided up, but that they may have
all things common, neither among them may be any that
lacks. He who does not (thus) gather with Me is a divider
of brotherhood and a breeder of dissension."

Between these commentators there is a gulf fixed, which
seems to make of the New Testament two books with
nothing in common, nothing, that is, in common about
social life. For this reason we learn more of what the
New Testament teaches and does not teach, by seeing it
reflected in the Fathers, than when we gaze at it directly
for ourselves.

Directly we turn to the Apostolic Fathers we are con-
fronted with a mass of social teaching, which no ingenuity
can explain away.

The Epistle of Barnabas, on the " Way of Light," says,[1]
" Thou shalt communicate in all things with thy neighbour ; thou shalt not call things thine own. For if ye are
communicants in the things that cannot pass away, how
much more in those that can ? "

This was caught up in the same words by the *Apostolical
Constitutions*,[2] with the additional clause that " it is

[1] xix. 22, Hefele's ed.　　　　[2] vii. 12.

appointed by God, that all men should hold the necessaries of life in common."

The Epistle to Diognetus [1] tells us of the brotherhood of the common table but not the common bed, of the imitation of God in His kindness, which is " not to overcome our neighbours, not to wish to have more than those who are weaker, not to grow rich nor to do violence to the poor."

St. Clement of Rome shows clearly what we may call the democratic spirit of the Church. " The more a man seems to be great the more he ought to be humble and to seek the common welfare of all and not his own." The true confession of Christ is " to be restrained, merciful, good, to be in sympathy with one another, and not to love riches." [2]

Indeed indifference to social wrongs is looked upon by St. Ignatius as a note of heresy. [3] " Observe those who are heterodox concerning Christ Jesus' grace, which came to us, how contrary they are to God's will. They have no regard for a love feast, none for the widow or the orphan, the oppressed, the bound, the freed, the hungry, or the thirsty."

It might be urged that Hermas [4] likens the Christian rich man to the elm and the Christian poor man to the vine, the former supporting the latter but barren in prayer, the poor man rich towards God for both. But this, read with what goes before it, on the positive perniciousness to the servants of God of owning houses, lands, or wealth in any but our own land, will be seen to be no real instance on the other side, but an attempt to turn the inequalities of the world to some spiritual account. In the Eighth

---

[1] Capp. v. et x.   [2] II. Cor. iv.   [3] *Smyr.* vi.   [4] *Sim.* iii. 2.

Similitude, too, the Master-builder squares the stones for
His temple by cutting off their riches altogether.

The whole Christian teaching in Hermas about almsgiving is so extremely explicit,[1] that one of the works of
absolute command, under pain of spiritual bondage, is to
rescue the poor from their grief and inconvenience, which
could then be done by bounty and benevolence alone.
This, with the little communes of the monasteries, where
all things were held in common, were the only things open
to Churchmen, for a long time, on the actual plane.   In
the next generation Irenæus, in his synodical letter from
Lyons, lays down the emphatic rule that, " In whatsoever
direction a man can do good to his neighbours and does not
do it, he shall be deemed an alien from the love of God."

As the Church grew and enlisted the educated men, the
debt to Plato became more and more frankly owned.
Much of his teaching was the common stock of thought,
and adopted by men who possibly knew nothing of the
bank from which it was drawn.   But the scholars, as early
as Clement of Alexandria, saw in the great exponent of the
common life the Attic Moses, who " prefigures the Republic
of Christ," as St. Chrysostom declared ; whose teaching is
" hardly ever alien from the Church," " whose disciples can
with very little change bow their necks to Christ," as
St. Augustine put it.   Indeed the criticism of Plato, and
the divergence from his teaching, which we find in Christian
writers, serves only to throw into greater relief the enthusiasm for what was accepted.

For instance, Clement departs from Plato on the slavery
question : " We must treat servants as we do ourselves,
for they are men, like ourselves, and God, if you consider

[1] i. 7, ii. 8, and iii. 10.

The Church and Social Problems

it, is equally the God of all, both to free men and to slaves."[1] Upon this subject St. Augustine teaches that slavery is as unnatural as sin, and that no Christian may own a man, as he would own a horse or money. Innocent I[2] declared that "nature bore men free, fortune made men slaves," and "a slave has such treatment as no man would inflict upon himself," and thus the condition clashed with Christian law—an argument which admits of yet wider application. Then again Clement, of course, fell foul of Plato upon the community of wives,[3] as Christian writers were all bound to do and did. St. Chrysostom adds a further contrast between Plato's city and Christ's. "His doctrine can only be understood by the learned, but labourers, sailors, and masons can see ours ; his plans are all city ones, but ours do in deserts also ; his way needs full-grown men, but ours even does for babes." In other words, the Platonic communism was never rejected, although polygamy, slavery, and exclusiveness were all challenged and rejected. Lactantius was inclined to quarrel with Plato's community of goods : he says that it is bearable about money, although "impracticable and unjust" ; but he is furious about the community of wives.[4] Yet Lactantius[5] is as zealous for equality as the Jacobins themselves. "God, who begat and inspired men, wished them to be all equal, that is all on a level." He also is equally desirous of the golden age, with its common property in land.

> "No right there was to peg or bound the plain ;
> But all men sought the common gain."

---

[1] *Pæd.* III. c. xii. 92, Klotz.
[2] *De vil. cond. hum.*
[3] *Strom.* iii. 2.
[4] *De falsa Sap.* iii. 21.
[5] *De Just.* v. 14 and 5.

God's Co-operative Society

" In that God had given the land in common to all, to lead a common life, not for wild and mad covetousness to usurp all things for itself nor to give to any what was born for all."

Another question upon which there is also a unanimous accord among the Doctors of the Church is usury. Indeed it is so well known how opposed the Church has been to this practice that the opposition only ceased in the days of the prophet Bentham. Renan [1] accuses the Church of putting back civilisation for a thousand years thereby. The subject is dealt with in Professor Ashley's *Economic History*, [2] but the moral question frightens our clergy into curious inconsistencies. If the Church has authority she has pronounced against usury. So has the Bible. So has the Prayer Book. So have all the men we quote as authorities. But the State allows it, civilisation (meaning the rule of modern commerce) is built upon it. Children are forced, by laws and policemen, to learn sums about it. Two seemingly contradictory arguments are evident to all men. The borrower of money, like the hirer of a cab, ought to pay his fare. The lender, who does not work, should not eat the labour of other men's hands. Most of us feel this to be an *impasse*, shrug our shoulders, and invest our cash in likely ventures. If we are cross-questioned, we get uncomfortable or abusive according to our piety or the want of it. Yet the only people who would square modern practice with ancient teaching are the reviled Socialists, who would solve the moral problem by making lending a State function.

If the assertion is correct, that the early Christians were entirely convinced of that associative principle which

---

[1] *Marcus Aurelius*, c. xxxii.　　　　[2] iii. 5.

The Church and Social Problems

includes what we now call Socialism, we shall find this
brought to light in the attacks of the Church's enemies
and the exaggerations of her heretics. This is obviously
the case. The persecutions took place under the law of
Combinations, which was drawn to protect the Constitution. They were political, against revolutionaries. The
Faith was objected to; as a *cærimonium illicitum*, it contradicted the spirit of the Constitution. The Apologists,
with one consent, point out that the Church was pacific :
Christ's servants did not fight, at least not with swords.
The first great reasonable opponent was Celsus, and his
grave charge was that both the Jewish and the Christian
religions had their origin in revolt, στάσις.[1]

This charge was cleverly made, for who can deny that
Israel came out of Egypt by a great brickmakers' strike ?
And the constant charge against Christians was that they
worshipped one whom the law condemned; and themselves
turned the world upside down. Origen's reply was a
challenge to Celsus to name any armed rising caused by
the Christians, and an explanation that Christ's law works
no violence nor does men to death. The defence really
evades the gist of the charge, for Celsus probably knew
that the Church did not appeal to that clumsy weapon
the sword.

With regard to the heretics, it is enough to point to
Basilides, Epiphanes, and Carpocrates, who all defined
justice as community, and advocated theft and universal
wantonness with all the violence of the modern anarchist.[2]
Land, wealth, and women, the last-named declared, could
not be held as private and peculiar, but were open to all

[1] Origen, *Migne,* iii. 7, p. 45.
[2] See Clemens Alex., *Strom.* iii. 2.

to seize. Since the defence was a vindication of law and of marriage, it was not the communism, but the inhuman anarchy, which was repudiated.

The equality of all men, bond and free, which came with the Gospel, was a common theme of all Christians. It seems to have been a levelling not of wealth and wits, but of social position. Origen [1] gives as his illustration, " As you can see in most of the orthodox churches, especially in large towns, the leaders of God's people take no precedence ; and they make no exception even for the most perfect disciples of Jesus." St. Chrysostom [2] seems to mean by it no more than that Churchmen should not give themselves airs, nor vaunt themselves over their brother priests and kings ; for he is careful to say that it does not mean there is no authority and no obedience. It came at last to mean no more (and no less) than George Herbert's first speech to his wife, when he assumed his canonical coat. " You are now a minister's wife, and must now so far forget your father's house, as not to claim precedence of any of your parishioners ; for you are to know, that a Priest's wife can challenge no precedence or place, but that which she purchases by her obliging humility."

The true character of Christian teaching can only be judged *ab extra* after the edict of toleration, when the Christian quarrel came out of the criminal courts into the schools. The fourth century might at first seem to be chiefly interested in the Arian heresy, rather than in any social questions. But the question whether the Divine Son was inferior to the Father, as touching His Godhead, had a very practical side to it, which was perceived by

[1] iii. 724. [2] *Eph*. Hom. xi. and xx.

The Church and Social Problems

the emperors, and made them keen partisans of Arianism. Modern students seem to imagine that their choice was a captious and haphazard one, and indeed part of that inexplicable interest in religion which so astonished the wiseacres of modern times. Politically the question resolved itself into whether the Society of the Divine Son was subordinate to the natural order of the civil life and its rulers. When once this is admitted it will at once become clear why the imperial Arians persecuted the democratic Catholics with such otherwise inexplicable fury. The great Doctors were none the less Socialists because they were defending the citadel of fundamental theory and not fighting merely for legal applications. The common fallacy that the Divine Word operates only in the sphere of the immaterial or at least of the personal life is roundly repudiated by St. Athanasius. He does not look to some ready-made hereafter to reward the cowards who despair of God's purpose here. He goes out of his way to tell us [1] that " the work of atonement would be incomplete and Christ not have received His due, unless all things were given to Him, including food and rest for the workers and burden-bearers ; and that if we did not have rest and food the primal curse would not be removed."

St. Basil the Great came of a rich and powerful house, and refused his friend Julian's invitations to court, not because he had no political teaching to offer, but because, at the time, he considered that this would be more effectively carried out in preaching, almsgiving, hospitals, and monastic communes. He never concealed that " the Word calls us to Socialism ($\tau\grave{o}$ $\kappa o \iota \nu \omega \nu \iota \kappa \grave{o} \nu$), brotherly love and obedience to Nature, for man is a political and gregarious

[1] Migne's *Athan.* i. p. 212.

animal. So in the common polity and mutual society, generosity is a necessity for the uplifting of the needy." Under all the ceaseless insistence upon almsgiving lies the Christian doctrine of the injustice of the world and God's purpose for a better state and a juster order.

A fair specimen of this may be taken from St. Basil [1] "The harshest form of covetousness is not even to give things perishable to those who need them. What injustice do I do, by keeping my very own ? Tell me, what is your own ? whence did you get it and have it for your living ? It is exactly as if a man seized a theatre seat and drove off all who came to it, claiming as his private property what is granted for the common use of all. Such exactly are the rich. They pounce upon the common heritage and make it private by their pre-occupation. But if every man took but what sufficed for his own need, and left what is over to the needy, no one would be rich and no one poor. Did you not fall naked from the womb ? Will you not go back naked to the earth ? Whence came what you have now ? If you reply it came automatically, you are an atheist : you do not recognise the Creator, nor give thanks to the Giver. But if you reply, it is from God, tell me the reason of the gift ? Is God unjust to portion our living so unequally. Why are you rich and he poor ? Surely it is entirely that you may have the reward of a kindly and faithful stewardship and he the great guerdon of patience. But you, engulfing all in the insatiable maw of covetousness, fancy that you wrong no man, when you rob so many. Who is the covetous man ? He who stays not at sufficiency. Who is the robber ? He who carries off all men's goods. Are you not covetous ? Are you

[1] *Hom. in Lucæ Destruam*, 6 and 7.

not a robber ?   What you obtained for stewardship, you
profess to be your private property.   He who strips a
man of his clothes will be named footpad ; is not he who
fails to clothe the naked when he could do it, worthy of
no other title ?   It is the hungry man's bread you hold ;
it is the raiment of the naked you lock in your cupboard,
the shoes of the barefooted are mildewing in your house.
You have the money of the needy in your hiding.   All
those that you could help and do not, you are treating
unjustly."   The teacher goes on to point out that the
words, "Depart, ye cursed," were not said to a
robber, but " it is the unsocialist (ἀκοινώνητος) who is
condemned."

It would be waste of labour to point out that the life
of angels, as the monastic life was called, repudiated
private property, not as a temporal discipline, but as an
essential part of the better state.   One short extract from
St. Basil's *Monastic Constitutions*[1] will suffice.   " First
of all they must have, what is in its nature a lovely thing,
they must embrace a common life and common diet.   I
call community of life most perfect, wherein private property is wholly barred out, the jar of opinion is banished,
and all confusion and emulation and strife are cleared
away.   And all things are common—souls, opinions, bodies
with all that nourishes and serves them—God is common,
the work of worship is common, salvation common, the
spiritual warfare common, the labours common, the gar-
lands common, many are one and the one not a unity,
but a manifold union."

It is quite evident that this was no esoteric doctrine
for cloisters, for in sermons to the whole people[2] he holds

----

[1] xviii.   [2] e.g. *In famem et siccitatem*, 8.

up the communism of Pentecost, as a mark to be aimed
at by all Christians altogether.

The patristic, indeed we may say the Catholic view, both
of poverty and of slavery, is the same. These things are
not laws of nature and inevitable ; they are diseases bred
of sin, works of the devil, which the Son of God came to
destroy. This may be illustrated by a specimen quotation
from St. Gregory Nazianzen : [1] " Do let us remember
God's law, which is highest and first. He rains upon the
just and upon sinners ; and makes His sun to rise upon all
alike. He has prepared the earth, field, springs, rivers,
and woods for all the dwellers upon dry land : the air for
the winged things and the water for those whose life is
of that. He has given the necessaries of life to all jointly,
without limit or stint, not impossibly conditioned or legally
hedged, not prescribed by partition ; but He has bestowed
the same in common and richly, and has left no want
unsupplied. He respects the natural equality of rank by
an equality of gift, and displays the riches of His kindness.
But men must needs get gold and silver, and all sorts of
soft clothes and useless shining stones and all such matters,
which are the symbols of war and rebellion and tyranny.
With these they are stupidly puffed up, and close their
mercy against their kindred in distress, refusing to succour
them even with necessaries out of their own superfluities.
What blockishness ! what stupidity ! Whatever we do,
pray let us reflect that poverty and riches, what we call
freedom and slavery, and similarly named things are later
effects on the race of men. They are the common diseases
which have fallen upon our baseness, and the symptoms
of that. But in the beginning it was not so. He who

[1] *Or.* xiv. 25.

The Church and Social Problems

first formed man, made him free and a master, bound only by the law of God's commandments and rich in the pleasures of paradise. All this He wished to bestow upon the rest of mankind, who should spring from the first man's seed."

St. Chrysostom is the wittiest, raciest, and most effervescent of all the patristic writers. To him the words " mine " and " thine " are words of the devil.[1] He was well aware that Plato had sighed and given up the problem of the perfectly just state, because he could not see how eyes, fingers, and lips were ever to be communised. St. Chrysostom saw no difficulty at all. It is a reasonable sacrifice : it is Christ's politic ($\dot{\eta}$ $\pi o\lambda\iota\tau\epsilon\acute{\iota}a$ $\dot{\eta}$ $\kappa a\tau\grave{a}$ $\chi\rho\iota\sigma\tau\grave{o}\nu$) that members should be presented, as war-horses are provided for the use of the State, not to be reclaimed for private use.[2] He often expresses the resolute opinion that private property is the root of all Church disasters and checks. It is not for lack of miracles that the Church is stayed, it is because we have forsaken the angelic life of Pentecost and fallen back on private property. If we lived as they did, with all things common, we should soon convert the whole world, with no need of miracles at all.[3]

A most interesting passage from the sermons at Constantinople [4] may be cited, not only for its social but for its historical value.

" That is a lovely saying : Grace was upon them all. The cause of the grace was, there was none that lacked. This means the zeal of the givers was so great that none lacked. They did not give partly and partly husband : nor give all, but as their private property. They wholly

---

[1] *Acts*, Hom. vii.; *Ephes*. Hom. xx.   [2] On Rom. xii. 1.
[3] Hom. xxv. *Acts*.   [4] *Acts*, Hom. xi. 3.

cast out class distinction and began to live in great plenty.
They did it, too, with such great credit. They did not even
presume to give away by hand, nor to make conceited
largesse ; but brought it to the feet of the apostles and
let them be the stewards and made them the masters, so
that finally the gift should be communal and not personal.
This, too, was that they should not become vainglorious.
If this were done now our lives would be far happier, be
we rich or poor. It would bring just as much happiness
to the rich as to the poor. If you please let us describe
this only in words, and garner the happiness in this, since
you do not want it actually. It is quite plain from what
was done then that the sellers were not lackers, but they
made the poor rich. Very well, let us describe this now,
only verbally, and let all of you sell all you have and
bring it to a common fund. I am only speaking verbally.
Let no one hoot, be he rich or poor ! How much money
do you fancy it would come to ? I estimate (for it is
impossible to speak by the book) that if all men and all
women here parted entirely with all their money and
gave their lands, goods, and houses (I must not say slaves,
for they had none then or possibly set them free), they
would easily total a million pounds of gold, more likely
two or three million. Now tell me, what is the total population of our city, counting all sorts ? How many do you
grant are Christians ? A hundred thousand, and the rest
Greeks and Jews ? How many myriads of gold have they
got ? What is the sum total of the poor ? I fancy not
more than fifty thousand. To feed these every day what
would be the cost ? But when there was common table
and they were fellow battelers it would not be so very
costly. Ah, but what shall we do, you say, when all was

The Church and Social Problems

spent ? Do you really fancy that could ever be ? Would not the grace of God grow ten thousandfold ? Would not God's grace be poured out richly ? What is more, should we not have turned earth into heaven ? If there the numbers were three and five thousand and the thing succeeded so shiningly and none of them complained of poverty, how much better with so great a company as ours ? Why, which of them without, would refuse to contribute ? To prove that it is this separation which is costly and the cause of poverty, take a house, with ten children and a mother and father. Let her work in wool and let him bring out-of-door wages. Tell me, if they had a common table and had one housekeeping, would it cost more than if they were all separated ? It is plain that separation would be the expensive thing. If they had to be separated the ten children would want ten dwellings, ten tables, ten servants, and all else at the same rates. Is not that so where there are many slaves, they have one table just to cut down the expenses ? Division always brings loss, consent and harmony always bring gain. The monastery folk live now, just as the faithful did then. Which of them dies of hunger ? Which of them is not fed with abundance ? Ah, but now men are more terrified of this than of falling into a shoreless and boundless sea. If we put it to the proof, then we should get heart for the venture. How much grace do you think they had ? Then when there were no faithful save the three and the five thousand, when all the folk of the world were hostile, when they looked for help from no quarter, they yet dared the plan ; how much rather now, when by God's grace the faithful are to be found everywhere ? Who would then still be a Greek. I myself think no one would. It is by these means we should attract and draw them to us. Yes, if we set forward on this road, I trust to God it will be so indeed. Only hearken to me and let us carry out the matter systematically, and if God grant life, I trust that we shall soon bring ourselves to this constitution."

It would be tedious to heap up instances, either from these great doctors or from lesser writers like Asterius Amasænus, because the argument concerns the tone and spirit and not the temporal proposals of the leading Churchmen.

The audacity of the Greek intellect, the fact that Plato was of their race, and various other like explanations, have been put forth to account for the dissimilarity between the message of Churchmen then and now. But these ingenuities do not seem to explain away the Latin Fathers. These have exactly the same spirit. In whatever way else East and West are divided, it is certainly not in the social teaching of the Doctors.

The Church, according to St. Ambrose,[1] is herself the mirror of justice, " the embodied form of justice, all men's common right. She prays in common, she works in common, and she possesses in common."

Since it is sometimes objected (though how this is an objection it is hard to see) that the Fathers simply adopted the communal notions of the Stoics, it is worth noticing that St. Ambrose combats two definitions of justice current in his days, and applauds the Stoics rather than pilfers from them. " To hurt nobody unless provoked by injury "; this is traversed by the gospel. " To hold common or public things for public purposes and private for private ends." " Even this is not natural," he says.

[1] *Off.* i. 29.

The Church and Social Problems

"Nature lavished all things for all persons in common. For thus God ordered all things to be produced that all might have common sustenance ; and the land, therefore, should be a kind of common property of all men. Nature then produced common property, unlawful possession (*usurpatio*) made private property. In this they say that the Stoics agree that what is born of the earth was all created for man's use ; but men were made for the sake of men, to be able to help each other. Whence did they get this saying, but from our Scriptures ? "[1] The common ownership and use of the land in justice is a constant theme. Take his treatise upon Naboth. "How far, ye rich men, will your mad greed be strained ? Will you dwell quite alone on the earth ? Why do you cast out what is natural and usurp the ownership of nature ? Nature knows no rich men, she made us all poor." "The world was created for all men, and you, the rich minority, try to claim it for yourselves. Yes, not only the ownership of the earth, but heaven too, the air and the sea, is claimed for the use of the rich minority. This field which you infold in your wide possessions, how many folk could it nourish ? Surely the angels do not hold the vaults of heaven divided up, as thou doest map the earth with thy boundary lines ! " "Rich men, ye rob all things from the poor, ye harry everything, ye leave him nothing ; but the pain of the poor and more, you rich men have to bear." Alms to the poor are only a rough approach to justice. "It is not yours, that you give to the poor, it is his. What was given for the common use of all, do you alone appropriate ? The earth is all men's, not the property of the rich ; but those who use their own are fewer than those

[1] *Off.* i. 28.

95

who have lost the use of it. Therefore (in alms) you pay
a debt, you do not bestow a bounty." In the Book of
Tobias, he lays down the Christian teaching upon usury.
"Nihil interest inter funus et foenus, nihil inter mortem
et sortem." Dividends and death are one, capital and
capital punishment are the same.[1] It is hardly wonderful
that the late Professor Bright should admit with a sigh
the Socialist tendency of this great writer.

St. Jerome considers that riches always spell roguery,
and a wealthy man is always a knave or the son of a
knave. "All riches are born of iniquity and the spoliation
of others. Lying dogs the collection of riches, and the
hand that is used to lock up treasure chests has a false
tongue belonging to it. Truth breeds poverty, falsehood
riches." [2] He was very zealous for active labour among
Christians, and of course in monks regarded it as robbery
and sacrilege for private property to exist. The higher
life has always been held by the Church to be inconsistent
with having things of our own.

St. Augustine, preaching to the people on Ps. cvi. 42,
"They rebelled against Him with their own inventions,"
writes thus : "This is what He says above : they did not
abide His word. That is a poisonous word man gives to
man, to seek the things that are his own, not the things
which are God's. In his heritage, which is God Himself,
when He shall deign to give Himself to be enjoyed by us,
we shall suffer no straits with the saints of His Company,
by the love of our so-called private property. Yes, that
most glorious City of God, when she obtains her promised
inheritance, where death and birth are no more, will have
no citizens who rejoice in private fortunes, for God will

---

[1] Cap. x. [2] *Michϙϙ*, Lib. ii. cap. 6.

be all in all. Whoso in this pilgrimage yearns sincerely and burningly for that Society will always be used to prefer common property to private property, seeking not his own, but the things of Christ Jesus."

Similarly, when he comments on "a place for the Lord," [1] he points out in a beautiful passage that the place must be in ourselves. " The heart affords a place for the Lord, for there is one heart in the charity of all in union. How many thousands believed, my brethren, when they laid the price of their own fortunes at the apostles' feet? What says the scripture about them? Certainly they became a holy place of God, not only holy places of God apart, but all at once a holy place of God. Then they became a place for the Lord, and as you know one place for the Lord was in all. The scripture says they had one soul and one heart towards God. But many, not choosing to make a place for the Lord, seek their own, rejoice in their own strength, covet earnestly their private property. But he who would make a place for the Lord must not rejoice in private, but in common property. This is what they did. They took their private fortunes and made them common. But did they not lose all they had? Well, if they kept things to themselves, each apart, each would have only had his own. But when each made common what was his own, each had all of all the rest. Of your charity listen. It is because of private possessions that lawsuits, hatreds, discords, wars among men, riots, civil dissensions, scandals, sins, iniquities, and homicides arise. What about? About our private properties. Do we go to law about our communal possessions? We breathe the common air and all behold the common sun. Then blessed are they who thus

[1], Psalm *Memento Domine.*

make a place for the Lord, by finding no joy in private
property. . . . Let us abstain, then, my brethren, from
holding private property, or from the love of it, if we
cannot from the holding of it, and we then make a place
for the Lord."

In this, as in so many things, St. Augustine seemed to
tune the Christian pulpits. The same, or parallel senti-
ments, are expressed by the lesser writers for the next two
centuries, and then St. Gregory the Great, the friend of
England, concludes the line of the Latin Doctors. St.
Gregory had a particularly well-balanced mind. If he
tells us, in the story of Dives, that riches are very dangerous,
he points out that Abraham was also rich.[1] If he notices
that the Gospel call comes equally to all classes, he adds
that to each it comes in a different manner. If he points
out that men, who have heard God's voice, often defy the
powers that be, he is careful to show that they also burn
with charity towards those they rebuke.

Yet St. Gregory in his *Pastoralis Cura*, a book which
has always been a text-book for the formation of members
of the ecclesiastical hierarchy, speaks deliberately and
carefully of the theory of almsgiving. Since he was highly
renowned for his great benevolence, this passage is of
importance. It sounds the keynote of his life. Speaking
to those who are commissioned to teach the Faith, he says : [2]

" In one way must they be addressed, who neither covet
other men's goods, nor bestow their own. In another way
those who are free with what they have, but cease not to
seize other men's goods. Those men who neither covet
other men's goods nor bestow their own must be ad-

---

[1] *Mag.* Moral iv. 60–61, x. 41–49, vii. 53–54, &c.
[2] Pt. III. cap. xxi.

monished, that they should carefully bear in mind that the land, the source of their revenue, is the common property of all men, and for this reason its fruits are yielded for the common benefit of all. In vain do those think they are harmless, who claim God's common gift of food as their private property, or that they are not robbers, when they withhold from their neighbour what they have received ; because daily as many die of the perishing poor, as they have rations for locked up at home. Really when we minister any sort of necessaries to the needy, we only give them their own, we do not bestow on them what is ours. It is no work of mercy, it is a debt of justice we discharge. Hence it was that Very Truth, when He told us to be careful to show mercy, said : 'See that ye do not your justice before men.' In full accord with this opinion, the psalmist too says : 'He hath dispensed and given to the poor, his justice abideth for ever.' When he was reviewing lavish generosity to the poor he rather chose to call it justice than mercy ; because the gift from a Common God is wholly just when those who receive it use it in common. Hence Solomon also said : 'He who is just, will give and cease not.' These folk must be told too to consider carefully the barren fig-tree. The husbandman quarrelled with it because it simply held the ground. A barren fig-tree holds the ground, when the mind of the owner keeps without use what could be of service to so many. A barren fig-tree holds the ground, when a fool overcasts with his lazy shadow a place which another could use with the sunshine of good work.''

It would be difficult to say when or how this teaching ceased : it would not be difficult in the least to construct a huge catena of authorities to support it, through primitive and indeed through mediæval times. St. Anselm [1] shuddered at the name of private property. "Even reason taught him that all the riches of the world were made by one Father of all for man's common use, and that by natural law not one of them belongs to one man more than to another." It survived the Reformation. Queen Elizabeth's private Prayer Book of 1578 contains this prayer for them that be in poverty, translated by Ludovicus Vives :

"They that are snared and entangled in the extreme penury of things needful for the body, cannot set their minds upon Thee, O Lord, as they ought to do ; but when they be disappointed of the things which they so mightily desire, their hearts are cast down and quail for excess of grief. Have pity upon them, therefore, O Merciful Father, and relieve their misery through Thine incredible riches, that by Thy removing of their urgent necessity they may rise up to Thee in mind. Thou, O Lord, providest enough for all men, with Thy most liberal and bountiful hand ; but whereas Thy gifts are, in respect of Thy goodness and free favour, made common to all men, we (through our naughtiness, niggardship, and distrust) do make them private and peculiar. Correct Thou the thing which our iniquity hath put out of order : let Thy goodness supply that which our niggardliness hath pluckt away. Give Thou meat to the hungry and drink to the thirsty : comfort Thou the sorrowful : cheer Thou up the dismayed : strengthen Thou the weak : deliver Thou them that are prisoners : and give Thou hope and courage to them that are out of heart.

"O Father of all mercies, have compassion on so great

---

[1] *Eadmer*, i. 33.

misery. O fountain of all good things and of all blessedness, wash Thou away these so sundry, so manifold, and so great miseries of ours with one drop of the water of Thy mercy, for Thine only Son, our Lord and Saviour, Jesus Christ's sake. Amen."

Would a prayer of this kind meet with any response, say in the Upper House of Convocation or in the Free Church Council? Would it be used in any of the circles blessed by rubber booms and the antics of Marconis? Obviously not. Yet thoughts so widely, so deeply, so long held by the Christian Church ought to be not only tolerable, but intensely dear to the minds of Churchmen. It might naturally be thought that bishops and archbishops would bless the promoters of modern Socialism, would pray for them in public, subscribe liberally to their Societies, and insist that all who discuss such questions should do so in the light of the Incarnation.

Whither is our development leading us?

GEN. THEO. SEMINARY
LIBRARY
NEW YORK

CHAPTER VI

THE CHURCH AND LABOUR

THERE are, of course, two nations in every modern country. It is merely a truism to say this. But the Churchman, who stands for a City that is at unity with itself, must face the fact that he is fighting for the moment a losing battle ; for the two nations are drawing apart, industrially (which is dangerous), and mentally (which is disastrous). Everybody with a thinking cap can see that in the days of domestic industry a man could quickly own his own capital, be master of his own tools. In the early period of combined manufacture, the tools began to be more elaborate and more costly to acquire, and now they are so increasedly complex, that by saving from his wages, a weaver or a printer would have to live for several generations to be master of the capital which he uses, or rather which uses him. Moreover, he would have to be educated in business methods, as even our Labour members and Labour leaders are not, before he could use the capital which such fancy saving might give him. This complexity and skill is obviously growing not only yearly but monthly. That is to say, as all men must agree, the status of the labourer is diverging still more widely from the status of the owner and from the status of the director of industry. Not all the ladders we can devise will do more than exalt the wisest heads of the one nation to the

GEN THEO. SEMINARY
LIBRARY
NEW YORK

ranks of the other. This is the Tarquinian method civilised. It cuts off the taller poppy-heads effectually, but
less crudely. The one nation feels its power grow, the
other its power decay. Each draws apart from the other.
The former becomes masterful and sometimes incredibly
insolent. The latter becomes sullen, despairing, even
madly anarchic.

It is also a truism that personal relations between the
classes are now old-fashioned. Bassanio and Portia do
not beat Gratiano and Nerissa ; but then neither do they
gossip with them, confide in them, speak their language,
eat with them, nor, in a word, make friends with them.
The stately homes of England are week-end resorts, where
the new man from Change or Colony knows none of the
tenants by name, except the gamekeeper and large farmer.
The travelled and cultured manufacturer is served by
drifting gangs of workmen, whom he knows less and less.

Two forces still act as interpreters, Art and Religion.
But of these the ministers of the former are quite content
to interpret the rich to all men ; but the poor fare worse
and worse at their hands. Take drawing and painting.
Portraits, of course, are pot-boilers. Who ever paints the
engine-driver when he has the director as his patron ?
Does any single picture in *Punch* make the poor otherwise
than contemptible, half cretinous, and wholly ridiculous ?
Is there one picture in any of the exhibitions which shows
manual work correctly ? or the manual worker as the
strong, athletic, and graceful person he so often is ? Even
to notice the correct use of tools is a task too hard for the
draughtsman's eye. There is no Millet and no Legros ;
but men use cross-cut saws balanced on their heel tips,
or reap the wrong way, or hoe with straight arms. The

parlour-maid, it is true, is sometimes noticed with justice, because she is to be seen in the dining-room ; and the chauffeur, because he sits near the magnate. But what about the platelayer, or the drover, or the cook, or the factory girl, or the sewer man, or the stoker ? Take novels again, the only form of book which is really studied. Laying aside all sheer fancies, what do we see ? For every person like Mr. Pett-Ridge, who sauces his maids and plumbers with a deal of humour, not always correctly ascribed, or Mr. Jacobs, who loves a sailor, there are a thousand romances of the well-groomed exquisite, who has cash in plenty and marries the fair loafer in " a creation," with a huge dowry in her tobacco-stained but otherwise delicate white hands.

Then turn to the poets, who because they are generally minor poets are the faithful prophets of their time. Their exaltations, agonies, colour passages, and oglings are never concerned with men in the wet, the oil, the dust, and the smut. They are the passions and aspirations that affect men who have lunched on chicken and Burgundy. Mr. Kipling has a message, the poetry of the active life, as opposed to the poetry of contemplatives, neurotics, and sedentary persons of all kinds. He is forced, by consistent thought, to see and to sing seven men from all the world, soldiers, explorers, service men, and bushwhackers. All honour to him for what he affirms ; but there are vast regions he has never explored, no less poetic than McAndrew or the jolly mariners, regions which should be interpreted to all, and mostly to those who are travelling away from them.

The musicians are leaving the melodic for the harmonic, until a shortage of the raw material of their art, the ancient

The Church and Labour

melodies of their race, drives them to snatch stuffs from Laps, Fins, and Andamanese, if perchance they can find them, or if they cannot, from each other's compositions ; or in the last resort of all to eschew melody entirely, unless it be such as a guinea-pig hutched upon piano keys will make for them, especially if he has enjoyed a little preliminary vivisection. These works have not come from the people and cannot appeal to the people. They are not supposed to do so ; they are not meant to do so. They are meant for the non-productive " nut " and the non-producing woman of society, for after-dinner relishes, to be the spiritual liqueurs of jaded folk with much to eat and nothing to do.

The great nation, in short, is untouched by Art, uninterpreted by Art, and ignored by Art, with a growing completeness.

There remains religion to interpret each nation to the other. She has ambassadors always moving to and fro between them, with fenders to deaden the shocks and jars of the constant collisions ; with a message to denounce pride and insolence on the one side, fury and despair on the other ; with an aloofness, which gives a power to see the possible, where other men only see the actual : or to put the matter in its true light, to remind both sides that they do not belong to the capitalist fashion of this world, which must pass away (the sooner the better !), but to a world wherein dwelleth justice. How far are these ambassadors of the sovereign and suzerain state conscious of their duties towards the petty states which are drifting into a savage and suicidal war ? They almost wholly ignore these pressing duties, and are generally unaware of their unique position. There are more civil governors who know the gravity of the situation, who try to do justice indifferently and truly, than there are clergy who have discovered even that justice needs to be done in thought and heart, as well as in law and civil conduct. We have a class ministry. Decent men know and love their fathers and their friends of school and college days, quite rightly. The natural man who is lit with gospel charity must always be, by instinct, a conservative. He loves what he knows and wishes to keep it. But when he finds that the world he knows is flowing away from the fixed principles of heaven, that mere conservatism does not conserve, he is apt to become peevish, to waste life in vain regrets and uncriticised criticisms, to shiver and lose his head, to charge blindly at things he knows nothing about, and to furnish cogent arguments for the very flow which he deplores.

It is of the first importance that our clergy, the *ecclesia docens*, should study humbly and patiently the lives of the poor, which they do a little ; and the views of the poor, which they never do. Then they must themselves explain those views to the class to which they belong (in the ugly worldly sense of this word class). Before they improve the poor man's mind they must know it and tell it. Then it will follow that all the things which do or can protect the disinherited will be their delight. They will try to know and to understand Labour leaders (most pathetic of men, with all the woes of Moses and but a little of his vision). They will be openly in favour of the existence, strength, and health of Unions. They will support all laws, imperial or local, which make for the health and are against the helplessness of the governed. They will speak frankly about the sin of low wages, pigstye houses, contentment with bad conditions, careless passing by on the other side, selfish snatching of individual benefits. They will convict men of these sins, of which the burden is truly intolerable. It is not necessary for every Churchman to join a Socialist Society, because he has already done this in his baptism. It is entirely necessary for a great many of our clergy to join one of our Socialist Societies, because not to do so is sheer sloth, cowardice, and want of vision ; it is the ungirt loin, the unlit lamp, and a craven terror of the subscribers.

Yet neither Unions, nor Socialist Societies, nor political parties are always wise or heavenly minded.[1] It requires often more courage to call a Union short-sighted than to call the squire a vampire and the board of directors assassins and burglars ; to say that brickmakers should keep pact, than to say the masters are Sons of Pharaoh for breaking it, as some of the wild curates have been heard to declare. It is hard to tell the angry men that a harried farmer (who has sunk his capital in crops and stock and does not know what on and in earth his assets may be) may not be wholly a knave, because he does not promise to increase his wages bill by £50 per annum. Yet it may be just as fair to do so, as to tell the farmer that sixteen shillings is not a living wage. It is harder still to make both of these understand that when Jerusalem is built in England's green and pleasant land, there will be no wages and no profits at all, no landed estates, no rival classes, no combinations of employers or of employed, no dirtied streams, no hedged orchards, no underground scamping, no unsymmetrical dimensions. Meantime why should not both nations unite to fight against the outrage

[1] Nor yet, to do them justice, are the clergy themselves.

God's Co-operative Society

of this inhuman division? to transform a system of captivity, which truly impoverishes both nations, into a co-operative polity where that captivity will not be smashed but led captive to the universal Man, Whom now we seek and shall some day behold? To do so might be to recapture some of that joy in life, which is almost extinct in the richer nation and far too uncommon in us all. But apart from their great work as ambassadors of the better land, the clergy ought to be correcting the unworthy caricatures of the poor which fill the press, the table-talk of diners out, the art galleries, the bookshops, and the ignorant minds of those who never allow Lazarus to come between the wind and their plutocracy. They need not explain the virtues and graces of the well-to-do, or voice their aspirations and pleas, because these people have already four hundred prophets, the Court Chaplains of King Mammon, who are ceaselessly speaking in every corner of the City, with all the persuasiveness of all the Arts, and the monopoly of the Press. The clergy and the clergy alone can, if they have the grace of the Holy Ghost, not only hear the cry of the poorer nation, but can reach the ears of the classes and carry the truth to them. As priests they are and always have been bound to be ardent social reformers; but as modern priests they are now bound also to be interpreters. We have missions from public schools and universities to Bethnal Green and Southwark; we really need settlements and missions from Seven Dials and Hoxton to Oxford or to Eton. The fish-porters cannot well reach the perishing hundreds in the West-end clubs, nor the Railway Men's Union evangelise the sorely necessitous in the grand stands, badly as these missions are wanted. But even the most timid arch-

The Church and Labour

deacon or the panic-stricken prebendaries might bear witness to the patience, dignity, wholesome mindedness, bodily grace, and mental sincerity of their humbler (splendid word!) parishioners; until their less humble relatives and friends are something eased of the foolish fictions, which they imbibed with their mother's—patent food for infants. These fictions are dinned into their ears and eyes from their earliest days. They are assumed in conversation, mixed with the alphabet and the arithmetic table, kneaded into their bread, sung to them in concerts, and shouted in the press. The father of lies has never been so active in traducing the absent, because the poor have never yet in the world's history been quite so out of sight and out of mind as they have now become. It is worth while insisting upon this new and interpretative duty, because it is a modern one, lately developed and consequently seldom admitted, and still more rarely undertaken.

If this interpretation be the most fruitful present work for the clergy just now, it must not supersede, but rather prepare all men to listen to the call of justice. That call is perfectly clear and unmistakable. A great wrong has arisen causing a schism, a widening schism, in the human family. Its existence is denying and blaspheming the life principles of Christ's Co-operative Society. No Churchman can afford to be indifferent, under pain of being false to his profession. His spiritual advisers ought to ask of him, what he is doing weekly and daily, towards reducing this national debt of the City of God.

Suppose that he replies that he is fully persuaded that neither by legislation nor by any form of civil action can the position, the relative *position* of the greater nation be altered, but that the *conditions* alone can be improved, then those who have the charge of his soul must not let the matter rest here. They must ask who can improve those conditions?—the whole nation, the smaller nation, the rich alone, or the larger nation by themselves? If our lamentable but honest conclusion is that the position of the poor has now and suddenly become stereotyped and incorrigible, then all our energies must be devoted towards these conditions. To express our disbelief in Socialism may be a very pretty way of saving spiritual trouble, of making a smart retort to the upbraidings of conscience, of refusing to render an account of our lives which Christians ought to be always doing, and which, some day, we shall all be compelled to do, when auricular confession is compulsory, at Doomsday.

The organs available for improving the conditions of the people being *ex hypothesi* three, the channels of alleviation are : (1) The State, which by legislation and administration through all its branches may enforce or supply decent houses, wholesome food and drink, fit medicine and medical treatment, the abatement of nuisances, dangers and disorder, access to free air, sunlight and the sea, protection against violence, robbery, and much cheating. It may see that no citizens are starved in mind or in body, nor poisoned or infected from known and resistible sources, that each may discover the work which belongs to his power and all may plead freely for what they think to be just. Even within these limits, what a wide field is opened for honourable work, in every centre and department of civil rule ! And also what a world of shams and jobbery, of place-making and fruitless inspection, of insolence and servility, of petty tyranny and blackmail, dogs even real effort ! and how many false and misleading attempts there

The Church and Labour

always are to divert the advance of united amelioration !

(2) If this bettering of conditions is to be the work of the
smaller nation alone, that means that we are to trust to
benevolence and alms ; to the high sense of honour, which
makes a landlord ashamed to own bad cottages and slums,
a colliery company to see that there is no overcrowding,
causes a brewer to see that his tied houses are orderly and
the drink honest, a mistress that her maid is happy in a
cheerful room, with reasonable hours, not lonely, unamused,
baited, and neglected. It means that alms will be given
with the utmost generosity and wisdom, that benevolent
Societies will be examined with minute care and then
supported generously ; that the minds of employés, as
well as their teeth and skins, will be the employer's care ;
that a serious attempt will be made to share the rich
things of art, music, literature, and amusements with the
other nation, not to keep them down, but to lift them up.
If the great delight of religion be also presented to them,
it will not be as an organ of criminal law, but with the
full knowledge that even the Ten Commandments were
given to set men free, and that the Sacraments themselves
are proofs and pledges of a splendid equality and a democratic unity. The more men profess their despair in " the
life of the world to come," the *venturum sœculum*, the more
they must be held inexcusable, if they fail in any of these
directions. Even in the matter of direct and private alms,
it is impossible to wait for amateur detectives to ask nine-
and-forty questions, to hunt up " the history of the case,"
while the cupboard is bare. Better it is, says Fuller, that
nine drones be fed than one bee starved. Our mathe-
matical rage for statistics allows Lazarus to go without his

111

crumbs while we are tabulating his sores and recording the number, breed, and sporting capacity of the dogs which lick him, so many licks *per diem*. There is only one thing which any man can give to another, and that is an opportunity. "What signifies," someone said to Dr. Johnson, "giving halfpence to common beggars? they only lay it out in gin and tobacco." "And why should they be denied such sweetness of their existence?" says Johnson. "It is surely very savage to refuse them every possible avenue to pleasure, reckoned too coarse for our own acceptance. Life is a pill which none of us can bear to swallow without gilding; yet for the poor we delight in stripping it still barer, and are not ashamed to show even visible displeasure, if ever the bitter taste is taken out of their mouths."

(3) There are some people, who are both impatient of the efforts of the Commonwealth and also of the benevolent well-to-do, even in the minor task of securing better conditions for the larger nation. To them the old line is exclusively true, "Who would be free, themselves must strike the blow." The kingdom of Heaven must first come within us, before it comes among us, they suppose. This certainly is not usually God's way of dealing with us all. We do not first study digestion and then dine, first know oxygen and nitrogen and then breathe, nor in ordinary life give this preponderating place to the intellect. But there are cases, where whole classes of men have been convinced that their opportunities were too few, and have enlarged them, by joint enterprise. The enormous power of the medical body is an instance; but they were aided by a state monopoly. The Jews have won toleration and power; but they are a nation, not a class. The serfs

The Church and Labour

attained a somewhat better condition through, rather than by, the revolt of A.D. 1381; but serfdom lingered until Elizabeth's reign, and only vanished because it had served its purpose. Class struggles, purely class struggles, do not seem to have been very successful for long, unless, as in the case of the middle classes of the Civil War and the bourgeois of the French Revolution, they seized political power first. But many things are now possible, which hitherto have never yet been. If a man has decided that even the conditions of the greater nation can only be bettered by that nation, he must throw his energies into popular education and instruction. He must solve the problem of how to give middle class business and organising capacity to large bodies of men and yet keep them from leaving the working class ranks; or how to get those who already have this training, to accept commissions and obtain confidence in the great labour army. He must have a robust belief in Trades Unions and their future development and discipline. He must wish for and try to obtain fuller ranks for each individual Trades Union and the co-ordination of each Union with each other. He must not be aghast at the follies and mistakes, which expose the army to assault: at the disheartening way in which the leaders are treated so often by their followers. There is no more difficult task than that of Labour leader. A first-rate and intelligent man is taken from the ranks. His money comes in irregularly. His home life gets upset. He has a thousand new temptations. He does not have power in proportion to his responsibility. A mistake or a defeat exposes him to fiercer enemies behind than he has in front. He is a marked man, and cannot return to what he was. The outsiders and thoughtless people denounce

H

God's Co-operative Society

him as an agitator, and believe he has originated all the trouble, which he is struggling to amend and appease. If he cannot by sheer personality and persuasion order his forces as deftly as if he were a traffic manager of a railway, his defects are roared into the ears of his supporters, who easily believe themselves to be sold and betrayed. The fierce light that beats upon a throne is lambent to the dazzle shed upon him. Yet for all these things, the Union leaders of England have been patient, capable, and orderly men, of whom our race may well be proud. They have attained, by the reasonable principle of co-operative bargaining, by their wisdom and moderation, not only a better subsistence for large bodies of our fellow-men, but have stood between them and the madness of despair, the cruelty of revenge, and the waste of disorder. Just now, when there seems to be a great driving movement of employers, aided by foolish (or designing) legislators, to destroy or paralyse the Unions, so selfish and shortsighted a policy may well cause, not only religious men, but even patriotic heathen, to espouse the Union cause with resolution and vehemence.

These three directions for work and hope represent three alternatives, one of which at least must be accepted by any active man, who is prepared to submit himself to the plain teaching of Christ and His Church. In reality they are not mutually exclusive. The sharp antithesis between position and conditions (it is William Morris' phrase) is only a matter for the reason rather than for the understanding. When conditions are improved (and it is in the power of man to improve them) position slowly alters or can alter. "Until we have fed the hungry, there is no power in us to inspire the unhappy." Yes, but when the hungry is fed he may, or may not, get the

114

The Church and Labour

inspiration which is more than bread. Amelioration, palliation, good conditions (who has not seen them in the colonies ?), are poor things enough, if that is the end ? The hygienic man, void of microbes, and filled with distilled water, standard bread, biology, and the glee of chess problems, even if he lives to be ninety and is buried in wicker, has reached conditions, for which it is worth no man's while to die or to live. Labour problems cannot even be stated correctly, let alone solved, unless we mean that man ought to have the extreme delight of knowing God and with Him be freely given all things.

CHAPTER VII

THE DEVELOPMENT OF THE CHURCH

"WITH respect to evolution," says Mr. F. H. Bradley,[1] "I may remark in passing that though this word may of course be used to stand for anything whatever, yet for all that it has a meaning of its own, which those who care to use words, not merely with *a* meaning, but also with their meaning, would do well to consider. To try to exhibit all that is contained in it would be a serious matter, but we may call attention to a part. And first 'evolution,' 'development,' 'progress,' all imply something identical throughout, a subject of the evolution, which is one and the same. If what is there at the beginning is not there at the end, and the same as what was there at the beginning, then evolution is a word with no meaning. Something must evolve itself, and that something, which is the end, must also be the beginning. It must be what moves itself to the end, and must be the end, which is the 'because' of the motion. Evolution must evolve itself to itself, progress itself go forward to a goal which is itself, development bring out nothing but what was in, and bring it out, not from external compulsion, but *because* it is in.

"And further, unless what is at the end is different from that which was at the beginning, there is no evolution. That which develops, or evolves itself, both is

---

[1] *Ethical Studies*, p. 173, *n*.

116

and is not. It is, or it could not be *it* which develops and which at the end has developed. It *is not*, or else it could not become. It becomes what it is; and if this is nonsense, then evolution is nonsense.

"Evolution is a contradiction, and, when the contradiction ceases the evolution ceases."

If we apply these weighty words to the evolution of a butterfly from an egg, an acorn from an oak, and ourselves from a spermatozoon, we shall approach the subject of the development of the Church in a humbler and more salutary spirit than is usual; for some people seem to think that the Catholic religion is like an old cope, which bargain-hunters buy and cut up into petticoats or sofa-cushions as their tastes suggest. We have, in fact, to do with a living organism, which has developed itself, is developing itself, and indeed must grow to live, quite as much as it lives to grow. The Word has still many things to say to us, which perhaps we cannot now bear, and those things are inset in the whole body, not in the formulæ exclusively, nor in the minds of the clergy, nor in the thoughts of the devout. They are: and they are not, for they are becoming. When the butterfly egg takes legs and walks, when the caterpillar sinks to a mummy, when the mummy bursts into a butterfly, there will always be eggs, caterpillars, and chrysalises, which shiver and repine; that is supposing they have wits enough to notice what is afoot. The Lord of life is working, and brings new things, as well as old, out of His treasury.

Let us take an example of development from the Psalm of the Saints.[1] There is a Hebrew root *dabar*, which means to put things in a row—stones, for instance. Thence it

[1] *Beati immaculati*, cxix.

passes to mean " to order, to guide, and to subdue." But to put sounds in order is to speak, notes in order is to sing, thoughts in order is to reason, reasons in order is to be wise, and so we get from a row of pebbles to the right hand of God Himself, and Deborah becomes the name of the prophetess who sets things straight for Him. Take the verses where this comes, and see what is really there ; although no one need suppose that the Psalmist, or anyone else at the time, saw the outcome of what he said.

(Verse 2) " Wherewithal shall a young man cleanse his way : even by ruling himself after Thy word." The word then is a rule of life. (16) " My delight shall be in Thy statutes : and I will not forget Thy word." It is the inwardness of the Law. (17) " O do well unto Thy servant ; that I may live and keep Thy word." It is the reward of life. (25) " My soul cleaveth to the dust : O quicken Thou me, according to Thy word." It is the source of life. (28) " My soul melteth away for very heaviness : comfort Thou me according unto Thy word." It is the restorer of life. (42) " So shall I make answer (or say a word) to my blasphemers ; for my trust is in Thy word." It is a shield and refuge. (43) " And take not the word of Thy truth utterly out of my mouth : for my hope is in Thy judgments." It is a prized possession. (49) " O think upon Thy servant, as concerning Thy word : wherein thou hast caused me to put my trust." It is man's plea with God. (57) " Thou art my portion, O Lord : I have promised to keep Thy law (or words)." It is one, given in many. (65) " O Lord, Thou has dealt graciously with Thy servant according unto Thy word." It is the guerdon of service. (74) " They that fear Thee will be glad when they see me : because I have put my trust in Thy word." Here it is the bond of a common faith. (81) "My soul hath longed for Thy salvation : and I have a good hope because of Thy word." It is the pledge and earnest of salvation. (89) " O Lord, Thy word endureth for ever in heaven." It is beyond time. (101) " I have refrained my feet from every evil way : that I may keep Thy word." It is a human trust, which explains morality. (105) " Thy word is a lantern unto my feet and a light unto my paths." It saves tripping and wandering. (107) " I am troubled above measure : quicken me, O Lord, according to Thy word." It restores to life. (114) " Thou art my defence and shield : and my trust is in Thy word." It is safety and courage in battle. (130) " When Thy word (plural) goeth forth it giveth light and understanding to the simple." Here the heavenly thing becomes manifold and dwells with mean persons. (139) " My zeal hath even consumed me : because mine enemies have forgotten Thy words." Here again the word, now manifold, gets slighted. (147) " Early in the morning do I cry unto thee : for in Thy word is my trust." It is the channel of prayer. (160) " Thy word is true from everlasting : all the judgments of Thy righteousness endure for evermore." It is as eternal as God. (161) " Princes have persecuted me without a cause, but my heart standeth in awe of Thy word." It is more to be reverenced than the powers of the world. (169) " Let my complaint come before Thee, O Lord : give me understanding (or cause me to think) according to Thy word." It is the ideal man, the great exemplar, myself raised to the highest power.

Now in these psalm verses we have St. John's epitome in embryo and the Christian gospel complete in all its members. Yet it is only after-events which allow us to see what surely may fairly be gathered from the spiritual principles which are here collected. So the Gospel itself is a development. It was always there, yet not always seen to be there.

So, just as St. John saw and showed what was already there in David,[1] so it is quite easy to suppose, or rather impossible not to suppose, that great fruits are still in the sap of the Christian tree, and will be produced in due season. We cannot turn a handle and hasten this production, for the Church is not a sausage-machine, where refuse treated with energy will produce savoury viands. But we can remove alien bands, which prevent the free circulation of the seasonable sap. We can, for instance, both tolerate and smile at those scarecrows of the clergy, the Higher Criticism, Modernism, verdicts of science, voices from Egyptian or Teutonic dust-heaps, M. Bergson, prosaic assaults upon miracles, the buzz of sects, and new (but half) baked theology.

In spiritual debate the opponent has always to be met with his own weapons : criticism by better criticism ; philosophy by better philosophy ; laughter by better laughter. Instead of fussing about the architects of the Old Testament (of which we swore to believe but a single verse and that the first one), we can enjoy what we choose of it. If we are wise we shall extract the eternal element, and not lose our tempers because facetious persons conclude that Ussher's dates are misplaced and that combined generations trade under single names.

Some omniscient (though hardly modern) inquirers have discovered that parthenogenesis is impossible, and others

---

[1] By which name is merely meant the psalmist, until the Higher Critics discover the author's real name and agree upon it.

feel quite sure that Christ is not risen. These dogmatic gentlemen of course will hardly expect the Church of an earthborn and death-vanquished Saviour either to develop or indeed to live at all. They will not be so illiterate as to expect, as a development, such a change as would take " not " out of the Commandments and clap it into the creeds. It is not truly the development, which they can demand logically, but the destruction of the Church. But supposing these people to be honest enough to stand aside, at least from this discussion, if not from the endowments of the Faith, it is perfectly plain that the Church does unfold herself, by presenting different aspects of that Faith for the criticism and the instruction of the world. This is done not by the advice and authority of those who might speak in her name, but by that interesting and inspired instinct of the whole body. Take, for instance, two things which have grown up lately, the great outburst of hymns and the harvest festivals. Hymns are never very much in favour with theologians. The Arians raised them to power. They are most abundant when spiritual life is at its ebb. They are often shoddy and unnourishing. But they have a kind of communal uplift about them : they shout the common feeling and rouse it. If they produce false excitement, pass about unsound notions and engender weak literary tastes, that is their abuse, not their intent. We have been forced from within, to use these stimulants and to provide them, because faith, hope, and charity have been in low health and are subject to swounds and anæmia. But the result is that the interest in religion and the demand for greater vitality is growing, out of all proportion to the silliness and nonsense of much that is contained in our hymnbooks.

God's Co-operative Society

The harvest festivals, again, are the people's desire, often actually disliked and discountenanced by the clergy. Some older men, now living, have boldly declared that the house of prayer shall not be turned into a greengrocery ; although the Father of all good gifts has not been squeamish about filling His world with kindly fruits. But on the whole, the body of the Church has prevailed against its brain. And surely instinct is here more reasonable than reasoning. We have not waited for our books of paltry doggerel to be authorised—we have used them. We have not waited for permission to be thankful for the harvest, we have been frankly and joyfully festive. Why ? Because the people have been dimly conscious that the producers and the produce, their work and their place in the world, need to be reconsidered in the light of the Incarnation. The bread, which feeds, has a sacramental value, a place in the Faith. It is an outward symbol of labour endured, of the skill of a thousand years, the embodiment of men's lives. That is what they feel and what they want to say. So that when there is inequality and shortage in parts of the human table, and the false prophets teach that this is inevitable and the fixed will of God, He, at least, may be clear, when He is judged, from the awful charge of inhospitality to His guests and from any desire or design to deprive them of any good things. Probably most ritual begins in this way, to lend emphasis to something ignored or attacked. At least we shall be safe to say that its appearance marks some evolutionary movement in the Church.

The plea, then, of the foregoing essays is not for making evolutionary advances in the Church, because conscious efforts in this direction are usually vain, and if they could

122

be effective, they would most likely be disastrous. It is rather a plea for observation, for taking into account and ordering ourselves for the developments which are coming from within, which are now made possible from without. It is a plea for what is there, and so can become visible and actual ; for what is not there, or it would not need to become so. It is not a plea for development, but a plea that the development which the wit of man has not contrived and the wisdom of man has not accomplished, should be recognised and welcomed : and further developments should always be expected and allowed for. Loyalty to the past is a fine phrase for a fine thing, no doubt ; but loyalty to the past was the keynote of Caiaphas, or he thought that it was so. Loyalty to the past would keep the ark of God in tents, when our own houses are of cedar and vermilion. It would have kept the Apostles all their lives upon the Mount of Olives, and the world would have remained in constant darkness. Loyalty to the past causes the keys of the kingdom to be so deeply respected that they are hung up in a museum and stared at. We call the museum a Church, and the staring, reverence. Modern wits suggest that the keys might now be put on the scrapheap and the bones of the Dinosaur, or the cheek-pieces of *Eoanthropos Dawsonii* used in their room. That is certainly reasonable, although not markedly loyal to the past. But neither side seems to be aware that there is a third alternative, that the keys should be taken down, oiled, and used. After all, they were not originally meant to be stared at, explained by custodians, and made into an excuse for collecting sixpences. The Church (it sounds irreverent and neologist to say so) was never meant for a museum at all. We are not expected to say, " What cunning

God's Co-operative Society

workmen the smiths were in the first century! What fine little intaglios were worked in the fourth century and called collects! How deep the heretic swords bit into this old armour of the Creed! Here is Cranmer's thumb in the Litany, and Charlemagne gave us this antique song of the Holy Ghost. The Communion of Saints is a doctrine which played an interesting part in the thirteenth century. There are St. Sylvester's initials upon the corporas. Most interesting, I am sure."

The visitors stare at all the treasures and the doctrines, the principles and keys, and are glad to have seen the curiosities: and then remember pressing engagements elsewhere. It is an intolerable audacity to suggest that mere oil and elbow-grease would bring these keys into use, and with such use they would open long-closed chambers and treasure-houses, yes, and gallant walks leading to fruitful fields; that the reopening of all these might lead to many kinds of interesting evolutions, not the last and not the least being that the museum would develop into a porch, an approach, a starting-place for great ventures and endeavours, for which it really was originally designed. This would be the true and only worthy loyalty to the past. It would give us some understanding of the present and some hope for the future. Because of the latter we should cease to hear that whining and weary note, which was the deep disgrace of the Victorian period. To be weary is one of the seven deadly sins (ἀκηδεια), quite as abominable as to be beery, and even more so, for it has less excuse and is no fun. As our spirits rose our ritual would also rise. We should cease to fear the drama in worship, and wonder why we ever were afraid of it. The truth is that not only is worship and every other communal act essentially dramatic, but even reason itself is the same. A man who thinks out a problem with closed eyes and still body has already erected a stage in his mind, where pro and con, the *dramatis personæ*, argue and fence, peep into one another's eyes, and even break jests at each other's expense. Particularly in public worship, where God is approached by and through men, there must always be a very marked dramatic element. That drama may be (it usually is) mounted with grossly careless stage management, with inattention to dress and deportment, with the pretence that we are so very spiritual that we can be dramatic undramatically, which means that we may act badly and childishly, so that we deserve to be hissed and pelted with figs. If this pitiful conclusion were pleasing to God, He would indeed show great favours to His sorry troupe. But no one can deny that these bad dramas weary and disgust men, who withhold their signs of disapproval because they know what the managers have forgotten, that He is our partner in the act of worship, and they fear lest the deserved scorn of the incompetent should light upon Him. Yet these very managers, so lacking in manly reason, in theatrical propriety, in the seriousness of the art they have undertaken, who violate the elementary canons of all possible public and corporate action, are the very persons who would recut the clothes of the Church, remodel what they cannot understand, and in the name of development would hugely impoverish the stage upon which they strut so clownishly. Therefore Prayer Book revision and many other desirable things are neither wise nor timely at present ; not because we do not need revision, but because we, much more sorely, need revisers.

Pope 29
Bible 34
Geo Herbert's wife 56
food for workers 87
Prayer for poor 100
Arcanum 87
Basil's monastic constit^n 89